DEMOCRATS IN EXILE
1968-1972

THE POLITICAL CONFESSIONS

OF A

NEW ENGLAND LIBERAL

R. BRUCE ALLISON

SOL PRESS
HINSDALE, ILLINOIS

438248

ISBN 0-913370-02-9
Library of Congress Catalog Card Number: 74-78096
Copyright 1974 by R. Bruce Allison
All rights reserved
Printed in the United States of America
First printing: April 1974

Published by SOL Press
107 Minneola Street
Hinsdale, Illinois 60521

JK

2317

1968

·A44

To Eugene McCarthy's idealism;
To George McGovern's foresight;
To John Nelson's tenacity;
To respectable liberals everywhere.

CONTENTS

PREFACE

My political confessions are in two parts. First is
a study of the events leading to and those resulting
from the establishment of one of the most significant
political reform movements in American history; a
movement which organizationally manifest in the New
Democratic Coalition. To my knowledge, this is the
only history of the national NDC organization ever
published. I am grateful to Governor Pat Lucey,
Marv Madeson, Midge Miller, Sonia Sloan and others
for attesting to its accuracy.

The second part involves my personal experience
as a volunteer and staff worker in the New Democratic
Coalition of Rhode Island. Rhode Island may be the
smallest state in the Union, but it will have its voice
heard. As one of the original states, it has participated in every Democratic National Convention. When
the Convention chairmen come to Rhode Island on the
decisive roll call votes, Little Rhody's delegation speaks
out as clearly and proudly as any. I feel privileged to
have participated in Rhode Island's Democratic politics.
In publishing my journal of those months, I hope to contribute not only to the readers' appreciation of politics
in that state but, perhaps more importantly, to their
understanding of reform politics generally.

As a journalist, I have remained faithful to the truth

as I see it. Yet, on a few occasions in the Rhode Island discussion, I have obviously withheld or abbreviated a name, doing so only in the case of an individual who, by taking no more than a marginal role in politics, retained, in my opinion, his privilege of anonimity. Hopefully, in reconstructing those days, I have offended no one. But if I have, I can only refer them to an earlier writer and publisher who dabbled in politics himself: "If all printers were determined not to print anything till they were sure it would offend nobody, there would be very little printed." - B. Franklin

NO MORE CHICAGOS

BATTLE OF CHICAGO

The peace movement came to the 1968 Democratic National Convention in Chicago already weakened by divisiveness and stunned by the tragedy of Robert Kennedy's death. Their dream of redirecting the Party to the goals of peace in Vietnam and human priorities at home came to a nightmarish end. By the hands of the old-line Democratic leaders they were muzzled, humiliated and banished from their own Party.

The progeny of the abortive "peace coup" within the Democratic Party organized themselves in the New Democratic Coalition after their banishment from the Party in Chicago. Existing on the fringe of the Democratic Party, the New Democratic Coalition worked for Party reform while maintaining its initial anti-War position and social change doctrine in hopes of eventually regaining its rightful place within the Democratic Party. Like many political organizations, it had a complex and troubled history. To understand the Coalition, its precepts, contributions and goals, it is necessary to return to its birthplace - Chicago in 1968.

The New Democratic Coalition was formed there largely in reaction to the inequities of the Convention system. It's battle cry four years later remained "No More Chicagos." The happenings in Chicago were essential to the frustration and goals which cast the mold of the NDC. The Battle of Chicago, in retrospect, can be divided into three stages: the committee skirmishes, the Convention floor confrontation and the post-Convention retreat to the streets.

COMMITTEE SKIRMISHES

The committee skirmishes were fought on several issues and were waged largely by McCarthy forces. There are four major committees within the Democratic Party: Rules and Order of Business; Credentials; Resolution and Platform; and Permanent Organization. There is also the Democratic National Committee(DNC) which then was composed of one man and one woman from each state, territory and district with a chairman appointed by the Presidential candidate or nominal head of the Party. The Democratic National Committee represents the Party between conventions, performing Party tasks such as the creation of special committees, appointment of sub-committees and preparing the Call to the next convention.

The clash between the New Politics and the old-line establishmentarians formally began August 19, 1968 with the convening of the Credentials Committee in the Conrad Hilton's International Ballroom. Earlier, a ten member DNC subcommittee, headed by Richard J. Dubord of Maine, had prepared a Temporary Roll Call of the Convention. Now, in Chicago, the one hundred ten member Credentials Committee, headed by Committeewoman Helen Gunsett of Ohio and the Governor of New Jersey Richard Hughes, would hear challenges and contests ultimately deciding the Permanent Roll Call of the Convention. Their decisions, in turn, could be and in many cases were, appealed to the full Convention.

The McCarthy attack force entered the committee
hearings exceptionally well prepared. Stephen A.
Mitchell, a seasoned veteran who had served as DNC
Chairman from 1952 to 1955, headed the operation.
Mitchell, along with Martin Gleason, a young Chicago
businessman, laid the strategy of confrontation. Under
the direction of Wayne Whelan and John Schmidt, a
task force of forty young and energetic lawyers had
been preparing McCarthy challenges since July. Oddly
enough, neither Mitchell nor Gleason were avid proponents of the McCarthy anti-War position. Both,
however, were deeply committed to the ideal of
Democratic Party reform and realistic enough to
understand the natural tendency of entrenched poli-
ticians to resist change.

During the summer Mitchell's legal task force
had scattered representatives across the country to
assist in organizing challenge delegations. For the
sake of credibility, it was essential that challenges
be initiated locally. The Georgia challenge is an example of this strategy. In July, three young, yet
seasoned, organizers, Sam Brown, Curtis Gans and
Dave Mixner, were flown to Georgia to assist Julian
Bond in organizing a shadow delegate selection convention. On August 10, 1968, the convention, held
in Macon, selected a forty-one member, racially
integrated delegation which was prepared to challenge
Governor Maddox's hand-picked regulars.

Gradually, the main thrust of Mitchell's strategy
developed into challenges based on alleged racial discrimination. Two men with great expertise in civil
rights, Joseph L Rauh, Jr., prime mover of the
Americans for Democratic Action(ADA), and Herbert
Reed, professor of constitutional law at Howard University and NAACP activist, entered Mitchell's staff
as senior policy advisors. They had a strong case

5

with which to work supplied them in part by the Party's own Call to the 1968 Convention. The Call required that all voters, "regardless of color, creed or national origin, " be given a chance to participate fully in all Party affairs. Governor Richard Hughes, the man presiding at the Credentials hearing, had, the previous year, while chairman of the Special Equal Rights Committee of the DNC, sent a letter to all state party chairmen reminding them of the Call's racial equality requirement. He pointed out that it was the Party's goal to see that all delegations "are broadly representative of Democrats in the state."

This Party position grew out of a compromise made during the 1964 Atlantic City Convention concerning the Mississippi Democratic Freedom Party challenge. The Freedom Party, a hastily gathered, predominantly Black delegation, under the legal guidance of Joseph Rauh, had challenged the segregationist regular delegation. The challenge resulted in a compromise permitting the seating of the regular delegation with a guarantee to the challengers that the '68 Call would contain the racial equality stipulation.

The '68 Call required further that each delegate be a "bona fide" Democrat who plans to participate in "good faith" at the Convention. This requirement was largely in response to the activities of those Southern Democrats who, during the '64 campaign, had failed to actively support Lyndon Johnson and in some cases had openly endorsed Goldwater.

Richard Hughes and his Credentials Committee were swamped with an unprecedented number(seventeen) of challenges and contests, most prepared by the reform-minded McCarthyites. Fifteen state delegations were challenged in whole or in part: Alabama, Connecticut, Georgia, Indiana, Louisiana, Michigan, Minnesota, Mississippi, New York, North Carolina,

6

Pennsylvania, Tennessee, Texas, Washington and Wisconsin. The Alabama delegation was actually challenged by two rival organizations, the Alabama Independent Party(AIDP) and John Cashin's National Democratic Party of Alabama(NDP). In addition, Alabama's state party chairman, Rubert Vance, filed a counter challenge against each McCarthy delegate. The challenges were based on racial imbalance, improper delegate selection procedure resulting in unrepresentative delegations, allegations of Party disloyalty or contentions that delegations failed to reflect minority views within the state party.

Mitchell's and Rauh's task force led pitched battles in several state challenges, particularly in those where overt segregationist practices made victory appear inevitable. However, they did not neglect the cases of unrepresented political minorities. In Texas they supported the Senator Ralph W. Yarborough faction in their challenge against the regular delegation of the iron-fisted Governor John B. Connally. The Minnesota challenge introduced the novelty of arguing for proportional representation on the basis of the Supreme Court's "one man, one vote" dictum.

The McCarthyites were occasionally on the defensive as in the aforementioned Alabama challenges and also in Wisconsin. McCarthy had entered Wisconsin in early spring winning a substantial primary victory April 2. In late May, acting under state law, he rejected part of the originally selected delegation replacing them with delegates of his own choosing. Consequently, the Wisconsin delegation, under the leadership of Donald O. Peterson, chairman of the state McCarthy For President Organization, was solidly pro-McCarthy. This to the chagrin of several old-line regulars.

When the sound and fury had passed and the dust

settled, it became obvious that very little had actually changed. At the conclusion of the Credential's hearing August 23, the Committee had decided in favor of one challenge, Mississippi, and had arranged compromises on two others, Alabama and Georgia. Mississippi's regular delegation was replaced by the integrated Loyal National Democrats consisting of moderates like Dr. Aaron Henry and Holding Carter III, the pro-Humphrey newspaperman. Each member of Alabama's regular delegation was required to sign loyalty pledges. In the event he refused, his seat was given to a loyal alternate or a member of the Alabama Independent Party. Georgia's regular delegation was seated along with Julian Bond's challenge delegation, Georgia's forty-one votes being divided evenly between them.

The unsatisfied challengers carried their battle to the floor of the Convention in the form of four minority reports filed for Alabama, Georgia, North Carolina and Texas. All to no avail, however, except to prove early in the Convention that the delegates were hopelessly divided on the most fundamental of issues. Although the McCarthy reformists were unable to crash the Party gate at the Convention they did get their foot in the door as reflected in the provision of the Credentials Committee majority report resolving that the Call for the 1972 Convention encourage state parties to ensure that all Democrats have a "meaningful and timely" opportunity to participate in delegate selection.

As lawyers conducted their protracted arguments before the Credentials Committee, another battle raged briefly before the Committee on Rules and Order of Business. This Committee, chaired by Governor of Illinois Sam Shapiro, held public hearings August 22 and 23 concerning, among other things, the fate of the

unit rule. Governor Harold Hughes of Iowa held the
banner for those insurgents calling for the immediate
retirement of the unit rule. Hughes had chaired a commission called into existence August 4, 1968 by members of the Credentials Committee and Rules Committee to investigate the delegate selection process and
Convention rules.

The Hughes Commission recommendations included
the immediate abolition of the unit rule in addition to
drastic revisions in delegate selection procedures.
Stephen Mitchell joined Hughes in calling for an end
to the restrictions of the unit rule. Opposing Hughes'
position was Frank C. Erwin, Jr., National Committeeman of the die-hard Texans who chose to make an
Alamo of the unit rule. As usual the Committee com-
promised submitting a majority report which prohibited
enforcement of the unit rule during the 1968 Convention
but not afterwards. This satisfied neither the Hughes
faction nor the Texans. Both submitted minority reports carrying the battle again to the Convention floor.

At last the reformers gained a close but decisive
victory. Their minority report, adopted August 27,
required one,"that the unit rule not be used at any
stage of the delegate selection process, " and two, demanded that "all feasible efforts have been made to
assure that delegates are selected through party primary, convention or committee procedures open to
public participation within the calendar year of the
National Convention. " This minority report of the
Rules Committee was similar in spirit to provisions
within the Credentials Committee's majority report
but more specific in applying those changes to the
1972 Convention. Victories were scarce for the dealers
of the new politics in the field of procedural change.
However, they did succeed in sowing the seed of reform in the Call for the 1972 Convention.

The war within the Party was fought on two fronts; the battle for procedural reforms fought within the Credentials and Rules Committees as described, and the battle for substantive policy reform. The latter was fought within the Platform Committee.

Representative Hale Boggs convened the first session of the Platform Committee August 19 with a plea for reconciliation and political tolerance. He was referring, of course, to the issue which had openly divided the Democratic Party since November and was about to tear the Convention asunder - Vietnam. The McCarthy/Kennedy/McGovern proponents of peace had aligned themselves against Johnson's war policy. In Chicago that policy had taken up residence in the Humphrey camp. John J. Gilligan, Senatorial candidate from Ohio; Kenneth O'Donnell, a Kennedy aide; and Fred Dutton, another Kennedy man, were the main architects of the peace plank. They worked closely with Mitchell and Rauh in devising a foreign policy plank which would free the Democratic candidate from the quagmire of Johnson's self-destructive Vietnam policy. The Platform hearings became an open debate on Vietnam: Secretary of State Dean Rusk testified on the inadvisibility of the Party establishing a position contrary to the administration's; Senator William Fulbright urged a dramatic turnabout in US foreign policy; Sam Brown warned that students would not work for the election of candidates who offered four more years of the same. At the culmination of the hearings, Johnson's strength was reaffirmed by a majority report which did not substantially deviate from the existing administration policy.

CONVENTION FLOOR
CONFRONTATION

The clash was carried to the unruly Convention floor during the August 28 session. A "peace plank" minority report was vigorously debated and finally defeated by a ratio of two to three. Resentment of the Convention officials' handling of this debate had been mounting rapidly and not without cause. During the previous session there had been a furtive attempt by Chairman Boggs and Carl Albert to push through the Platform debate at a late hour, past one a.m., to avoid prime time television coverage. At the next session, proponents of the peace plank were prevented from distributing pamphlets on the Convention floor. Then, during the vote, the band played martial tunes later increasing the volume to drown out the voices of the New York delegates who began singing "We Shall Overcome." The rift between the peace and Johnson factions became irreparable at this point. For the remaining sessions the Convention floor was a sea of storms. No one was in the mood for compromise.

RETREAT TO THE STREETS

The streets of Chicago were equally tempestuous. Allard Lowenstein, an initiator of the "Dump Johnson" movement and head of the Coalition For An Open Convention had canceled his mass protest plans after being denied a city permit for use of Chicago's Soldiers' Field. McCarthy and his student coordinator, Sam Brown, anticipating the worst, had likewise waved off the planned influx of student campaign workers.

However, others were not to be dissuaded. Under
the fatherly leadership of David Dellinger, the National Mobilization Committee to End the War in Vietnam (National Mobe) arrived in Chicago with its articulate student organizers Rennie Davis and Tom
Hayden. Another less political organization, Youth
International Party (Yippies), the fanciful creation
of Abbie Hoffman, Jerry Rubin and Paul Krasner,
was there to conduct a "festival of life" and to mock
the Democrats with the nomination of their own presidential candidate, Pegasus the Pig.

The Chicago policemen's brutal treatment of these
street people and the newsmen who covered their activities was the final outrage for the already discon-
tented delegates. The police violence in front of the
Conrad Hilton the night of August 28 was particularly
incitive of the delegates within the Amphitheater.
Senator Abraham Ribicoff's speech nominating the
Senator from South Dakota, George McGovern, ex-
emplified the confrontation between the feuding Party
factions. Ribicoff, enraged by the Hilton incident
which had occurred the previous hour, broke from
his prepared text, cast an accusatory stare at Mayor
Daley and stated that with McGovern as President,
"we wouldn't have Gestapo tactics in the streets of
Chicago."

Those of the old politics and those of the new were
now totally irreconcilable. Those who had worked
for McCarthy, Kennedy and a peace plank were effectively locked out of the Democratic Party in 1968.
Their response was varied. Some, like Marcus Raskin,
co-director of the Institute for Policy Studies located
in Washington, D.C., chose the role of renegade.
Raskin called a meeting at the Drake Hotel directly
after the nominating session, around one a.m., which
made plans for a fourth party. About three hundred

fifty persons, mostly McCarthy supporters, listened
to such celebrities as Gore Vidal, Paul Newman,
Jules Feiffer and Peter Yarrow.

About the same time, a large group of delegates
lead by Paul O'Dwyer of New York, caucused at the
Amphitheater expressing their unity in opposition to
the condition of the Democratic Party. The group
included speech writer Richard Goodwin, Congressman William F. Ryan of New York, Congressman
George Brown of California, Donald Peterson of
Wisconsin and Reverend Richard Neuhaus of New
York. They rode in buses to the end of Grant Park
and there led a candlelight march of about six hundred
delegates and supporters down Michigan Avenue to
the Conrad Hilton Hotel. Around four a.m. a group
of speakers including Goodwin, Norman Mailer,
Julian Bond and Monique Dzu, daughter of the impri-
soned Vietnameses politician Truong Dinh Dzu, addressed a gathering of the street people and others
in Grant Park. The delegates and the street people
were united in their common banishment and disdain
of the establishment forces.

The rebellion continued to grow later that day,
August 29. At eleven a.m. a fourth party was discussed further by Robert Lamm and about two hundred
persons gathered at the Conrad Hilton. McCarthy
was their candidate choice.

McGovern, meeting with his supporters, expressed
his optimism that the Party could be restructured,
saying that 1968 "may well mark the end of the old
backroom politics and the first birth pangs of the
new politics centered on people and principle."

The sense of banishment from the Party was felt
strongly by many delegates. At this moment, McCarthy,
speaking to his supporters at the Conrad Hilton Hotel,
greeted them as the "government-in-exile." Later

that afternoon he repeated the phrase as he addressed a crowd of dissidents in Grant Park. He exhorted the "government of the people in exile" to "work within the political system and . . . help seize control of the Democratic Party in 1972."

NEW DEMOCRATIC COALITION

Hundreds of dissident Democrats who felt abused and excluded, crowded into caucus rooms throughout Chicago the night of August 29 and the following day to discuss their plight. Raskin's fourth party strategy, though discussed seriously, never materialized, probably for lack of a willing candidate. However, another concept, later to realize itself in the New Democratic Coalition, was born in a caucus room of Chicago's Sherman House that fertile Thursday evening.

BIRTH OF THE NDC

About thirty persons participated in the Sherman House discussion. To their credit they did more than merely engage in reactionary rhetoric. They expressed their common committment to the restructuring of the Democratic Party and then took positive action by appointing a Temporary Organizing Committee assigned the task of planning a national organizing meeting. The committee, chaired by the late Jack Gore, Assistant Director of Labor Education at the University of Colorado's Labor Research Center, was composed of political activists who felt strongly the sting of banishment from their own Party. The committee included the following: John Cashin, Chairman of Alabama's National

Democratic Party which had unsuccessfully challenged their state's regular delegation; Allard K. Lowenstein, US House candidate from New York and spark plug of the anti-Johnson movement; Donald Peterson, Chairman of Wisconsin's pro-McCarthy delegation; Sanford Gottlieb, Executive Director of the National Committee for a Sane Nuclear Policy (SANE) and District of Columbia delegate; Earl Craig, a Minnesota McCarthy supporter; Ronnie Dugger, editor of the TEXAS OBSERVER; David Hoeh, candidate for the US House in New Hampshire and Chairman of that state's delegation; Milton Rosenberg, a University of Chicago psychologist; Arnold Kaufman, a political theoretician and philosophy professor at the University of Michigan; Harold Rosenthal, a Pennsylvania McCarthy delegate; and Frederick Tuttle, Jr., a Kennedy delegate from California. Others, including Julian Bond, Chairman of the Georgia Loyalist delegation and Paul Schrade, Western Regional organizer for the United Auto Workers, joined in the formation of this intra-Party movement.

With memories of Convention inequities fresh in mind, the Temporary Organizing Committee devoted itself to the task of solidifying the defeated, divided, disorganized and, in most cases, disparaged reform element within the Democratic Party. They established an office in Minneapolis and assigned Earl Craig, a Black McCarthy supporter the task of coordinating plans for a national organizational meeting to be held September 14-15, 1968. Craig and the committee contacted state leaders who had supported the McCarthy, Kennedy or McGovern campaigns, in addition to representatives of minority groups. In short, they contacted the dissatisfied elements within the Democratic Party; those who had a bona fide interest in seeing the Party restructured. Craig mailed three hundred invitations for the planned September meeting, then, realizing

more time was needed, postponed the meeting until
October. Some, however, still came to Minneapolis
for the September 14-15 meeting.

ORGANIZING

Those attending the September meeting prepared
an agenda for the October meeting, opted for maintaining the Minneapolis office and decided to hire
Craig as executive director of the organization which
they christened the New Democratic Coalition. Jack
Gore, speaking September 15, said that the NDC was
formed to stimulate "electoral reform for identification
with the needs of the people in . . . social action, "
and "to develop a major program for policy change
in government through the Democratic Party. " The
issues which now united this coalition were those
which effected them individually prior to the Convention - War, race and internal Party reforms. The
repression and insults they suffered in Chicago served
as a catalyst to bond these people together in a political structure.

More invitations were sent for the October 5-6
organizational meeting. At that time two hundred
forty persons representing forty states came to Minneapolis to present their views and seek agreement
on goals and activities. NDC emerged from that
meeting a viable, though not yet powerful, organization.
It set as its goals the revitalizing and restructuring
of the Democratic Party. Although they chose not to
break from the Party, it was resolved that NDC would
involve itself in electoral politics and reforms in the
capacity of a separate interest group. An organizing
convention was planned for 1969 and the formation of
a thirty-five member Temporary Steering Committee

was approved. Don Peterson and Paul Schrade were chosen to serve as co-chairmen of the Temporary Steering Committee.

The selection of Schrade and Peterson illustrated the desire to reunite the reform movement which in the struggle prior to the Convention had divided into the often antagonistic Kennedy and McCarthy camps. Donald Peterson had been an all-out McCarthy backer in Wisconsin. He was then vice-president of Wisconsin's Black River Dairy Products, distributors of Roma Pizza. With a history of participation in such organizations as the ADA he was well established in the ranks of the liberal movement. He even led a protest march composed of angry Convention delegates who staged an abortive "walk-in" to the Amphitheater August 29 in the wake of the Chicago Convention tumult.

Schrade, prior to Robert Kennedy's death, was a firm and powerful Kennedy supporter. As Western Director and member of the International Executive Board of the United Auto Workers, Schrade exerted considerable influence over that element of the electorate which served as the backbone of Kennedy's Presidential hopes. He was a young and energetic labor organizer who, while devoting time to anti-War protests, the grape boycott and campus activities, demonstrated his appreciation and understanding of Kennedyesque mass appeal politics. During the California primary campaign he became one of RFK's close associates and was with Kennedy at the moment of the assasination. That night, Schrade, along with four other bystanders, was struck by a bullet from the gun of Sirhan Sirhan. Schrade suffered severe head injuries which required several months of hospitalization; plenty of time to reconfirm his devotion to peaceful social change.

With the election of Perterson and Schrade, the

Kennedy and McCarthy factions were at least symbolically united under the banner of NDC. They called a meeting of the Temporary Steering Committee for the next month, November 24 in St. Louis. At that time the committee consisted of the following members: Bella Abzug(NY); Herman Badillo(NY); Julian Bond(GA); David Bordeh(NY); Thomas Bradley(CA); Sam Brown (IA);John Cashin(AL); John Convers(MI); Bert Corona (CA); Ronnie Dugger(TX); Harvey Furgatch(CA); Curtis Gans(DC); Jack Gore(CO); Sanford Gottlieb(MD); Curtis Graves(TX); Michael Harrington(NY); Gerald Hill(CA); David Hoeh(NH); Joseph Huert(AZ); Arnold Kaugman (MI); Allard Lowenstein(NY); Pat Lucey(WI); Robert Maytag(CO); Midge Miller(WI); Rudy Ortiz(NM); Albert Pena(TX); Channing Phillips(DC); A.A. Rayner(IL); Don Rothenberg(CA); Abe Tapia(CA); Adam Walinsky (VA).

Discussed at this meeting were the broad questions of Steering Committee composition, goals and finances. Resulting from the discussion was a Provisional Statement of Purpose which set forth the underlying rationale of the Coalition. It states that the NDC as a national organization strives for "a just and open society, peaceful social change, economic development at home and abroad and an end to the cold war and creative approaches to world peace." Such as collection of loosely worded goals was easily agreed upon by everyone and although saying very little other than that the organization was a liberal one, it did offer all members a sense of common ground. The important element within the Provisional Statement of Purpose and the one which made the NDC a potentially powerful organization was that concerning Party reform - the NDC "intends to transform the Democratic Party into a national political instrument which will represent and provide avenues of participation for all citizens." And as part of its strategy to accomplish this transformation, the Statement continues, it will "seek to elect enlightened and representative leadership on every level from precinct to Presidency." By concentrating on Party reform, an immediate issue, specific and realizable, the NDC enhanced the probability of maintaining its coalition and acting effectively.

Those who attended this St. Louis meeting had learned a great deal from their pre-Convention and Chicago experiences. Their divisions and disorganization had lost the Battle of Chicago. Now, tempered by defeat, they seemed to grasp the political truth that to lead the Party, one must control Party mechanisms. And that would require a consistent, concentrated and sincere effort by their national coalition. To this end the Temporary Steering Committee enumerated specific functions the NDC was to perform. They were as follows:(1) act as a clearing house for relevant political issues; (2) provide staff and assistance to select candidates; (3) identify and organize local leaders; (4) use task forces to develop future issues.

The next Temporary Steering Committee meeting was held January 18-19, 1969, in New Brunswick, NJ. Although an exceptionally young organization, the NDC appeared to be gaining strength and discipline rapidly. Earl Craig and Patrick Fallon had done a good job in planning the meeting around an all-inclusive yet orderly agenda. Co-chairman Paul Schrade began the proceedings with a national report followed by Executive Director Craig's report on the organizational status. Don Rothenberg presented the financial report. After an examination of these three critical areas, it was evident that the prognosis was good.

Pat Lucey (elected governor of Wisconsin in 1970) proving himself an influential and valuable member,

spoke on the arrangement of national priorities. Curtis
Gans, a young and knowledgeable political activist who
had proven himself during the McCarthy campaign,
spoke in tones of guarded optimism. He, like many
others, had gained a new political realism from recent campaigning. Sanford Gottlieb offered a progress
report on plans for the first national NDC convention,
a project initiated at the first organizational meeting
in Minneapolis.

Another significant item on this meeting's agenda
was John Garfield's report on the Party Reform Task
Force. At the earlier St. Louis meeting on November
24, 1968, Garfield had been appointed to organize an
NDC task force assigned the urgent job of considering
and implementing the mechanics of Party reform. The
Chicago Convention had adopted resolutions which called
for procedural reforms. These resolutions came from
the Credentials Committee majority report and the
Rules Committee minority report.

The NDC, realizing the integral role Party reform
played in its future, resolved to act as watchdog and
participant to assure that this mandate for reform was
not neglected by Party officials. Anticipating the
Party's appointment of commissions to implement the
Convention's resolutions, the NDC created Garfield's
task force to serve as a parallel reform commission
protecting NDC interests and contributing whenever
possible. Senator Fred Harris, then Chairman of the
Democratic National Committee did, in fact, appoint
two commissions the next month (February 8, 1969).
The two commissions were the Commission on Party
Structure and Delegate Selection, chaired by Senator
George McGovern; and the Commission on Party Rules
headed by Congressman James G. O'Hara of Michigan.
The NDC, exercising some political foresight, was
preparing to deal with these commissions.

The New Brunswick meeting also served as a forum for Arnold Kaufman, who spoke on education; Michael Harrington, author and journalist, also spoke discussing the urban crisis. Abe Tapia, President of the Mexican American Political Association, addressed the gathering instructing the Coalition on his interest group's particular needs and possible contributions. As demonstrated by the diversity of speakers, the NDC was seeking a broad foundation. The topics of discussion were the social problems which the new Democrats were promising to understand and someday solve. Yet the NDC at New Brunswick was concerned with more than just the future. It was prepared to act immediately to gain control of the Party mechanisms which would guarantee that the Party's future would be their future. Furthermore, as demonstrated by the emphasis placed upon the organizational reports, the NDC was concerned with day-to-day survival. The group was expanding steadily at this point and doing well enough financially to announce to the New Brunswick participants the opening of a Washington, D. C. office. At this time the Coalition claimed organizations in twenty-two states and anticipated new organizations in several other states.

Those present at the New Brunswick meeting included the following: Adam Walinsky(VA); Earl Craig (MN); Curtis Graves(TX); Bella Abzug(NY); Don Rothenberg(CA); Ken Tilsen(MN); Jim Lindheim; Mike MacDonald(NY); Bob Toal(IN); Blanche Mahoney(KY); Arnold Kaufman(MI); Betty Irwin(KY); Midge Miller (WI); Larry White(OH); Sonia Sloan(DE); Pat Lucey (WI); Sam Brown(MA); Abe Tapia(CA); John Garfielf (IA); Bob Paul(PA); Keith Garlid(MD); Louis Backer; Dolores Huerta; Dick Leone(NJ); Al Fishman(MI); Michael Harrington(NY); and John Nelson(RI).

The Temporary Steering Committee next met March 1-2, 1969, at the Hotel Washington located in Washington, D.C. Again a wide diversity of topics was on the agenda. The NDC was taking strong positions on a myriad of issues. Adam Walinsky reported on the Emergency Employment Act, legislation the New Brunswick group had endorsed as "a first step in providing every American with a decently paid job with a future." And at this time when anti-ABM fever ran high among most liberals, the NDC joined with other organizations in condemning the proposed ABM expansion. Sam Brown, an articulate Harvard Divinity School student, spoke against the reactionary repression aimed at campus dissent. He singled out the statements of Reverend Hesburgh of Notre Dame and President Nixon as danger signs in the rising tide of repression. Curt Gans submitted a resolution on the ever present Vietnam issue and Paul Schrade spoke on the grape boycott.

John Garfield was able to speak optimistically of progress in Party reform. With his vice-chairmen, Martin Dworkin of Minnesota and Keith Garlid of Maryland, he submitted a comprehensive report describing the function and organization of his task force. Although plans were made for the establishment of a paid staff, funded through NDC, consisting of twenty-five members including the experienced Ann Wexler of Connecticut who had served on the Rules Committee during the '68 Convention, this task force never really got off the ground. Mutiple problems which were soon to overtake the NDC squelched this seemingly well planned effort.

Dr. John Cashin, leader of the National Democratic Party of Alabama, found strong support among those attending the NDC meeting. It was the consensus that Cashin's group receive the endorsement of the NDC in its bid for representation on the Democratic National Committee. The following summer, Don Peterson and Earl Craig attended the July 12, 1969, NDPA convention in Greene County on behalf of the NDC, again demonstrating the Coalition's belief that the future of the Democratic Party in the South rested largely with the Black constituency. At the Washington meeting, the NDC also endorsed the representation of Julian Bond's Loyal Democrats of Georgia in the Democratic National Committee instead of Governor Lester Maddox's regular Democrats.

HOLDING ON

At this point the NDC was an expanding intra-Party movement which served as a rallying point for a growing number of dissidents. The issues were many and varied forming a broad base which the Coalition needed to survive. However, the NDC had somewhat over-extended itself as the following financial report submitted March 1, 1969, attests:

Income:
Registration fees at the
   Minneapolis meeting -   2450.00
State group contributions
   (TX; WI; IN; MI; MO) -   1600.00
Contributions over $250
   (seven persons) -   5250.00
Other contributions -   4666.32
Total   13966.32

Expenses:
Salary -   3965.00

24

Travel (Staff, $1138.20 and	
Steering Committee, $1908.97) –	3040.17
Meeting costs;	
Minneapolis	1510.97
St. Louis	69.44
New Brunswick	106.46
Press conference in D.C.	89.10
Equipment and supplies –	1153.65
Rent and utilities –	2711.77
Advance for NEW REPUBLIC ad	450.00
Misc. –	100.00
Total	13192.56
Account balance:	773.76
Liabilities:	
Phone bill due March 10 –	1020.00
Rent, utilities, office –	215.00
Salary –	4145.00
Expenses –	434.00
Travel (staff only) –	450.00
Total	6214.00

No organization, no matter how noble its purpose or how needed its service, can long exist with such a considerable debt (the US government excluded). Fund raising must always receive top priority in all political organizations. To solve their financial problems the Temporary Steering Committee chose to conduct a fund raising dinner in Washington, D.C. Pat Lucey was appointed Dinner Committee Chairman.

The NDC sponsored one hundred dollar a plate dinner was held May 4, 1969, at the Sheraton Park Hotel. It was the NDC's first national fund raiser and a highly successful one. The three main speakers, Senators Edward Kennedy, Harold Hughes and George McGovern, attracted a great deal of press coverage as they spoke to an audience of over five hundred persons. Kennedy spoke against the War, while Hughes, a favorite of NDC because of his early interest in Party reform, spoke against those elements of the Party system which hindered popular participation in Party affairs. Hughes spoke to a receptive audience when he said, "the truth is that our political parties have become corroded, boss-oriented and neither accessible nor responsive to the rank and file of the constituents of America."

Pat Lucey happily reported the success of the fund raising dinner at the Temporary Steering Committee meeting held May 25, 1969, again in Washington, D.C. Through the efforts of Lucey and the Dinner Committee including Adam Walinsky, Blair Clark, Jack Gore, Midge Miller and Don Green, the NDC had made a net profit of $16,000. At the same time, however, Executive Director Earl Craig announced a pre-fund raising dinner debt of $16,084.31 and a bank balance of $111. So, if nothing else, the NDC was still solvent.

Some organizational problems were beginning to beset the Coalition, however. Earl Craig announced his resignation as executive director effective May 31, 1969, with the admonition that the NDC was in need of a well-paid national staff and greater financial support. Co-chairman Don Peterson, accepting Craig's resignation, immediately appointed a Hiring Committee to select a replacement. The committee included Adam Walinsky, Arnold Kaufman, John Cashin, Rudy Ortiz. Sonia Sloan, Don Peterson, Paul Schrade, Sam Brown and Blair Clark.

The assembled group, aware of their intense financial problems, named Blair Clark as treasurer and chairman of the financial committee to seek donations. Clark seemed the ideal choice for the job. An independently wealthy man himself, he had come in contact with many influencial persons during his career as a newspaperman and CBS executive. His close friends included the late President Kennedy and the poet Robert Lowell who dedicated a book to him. He served as a press aide to Averell Harriman during his successful 1953 gubernatorial campaign. And then in late 1967 he took command of the McCarthy Presidential bid, serving as campaign manager for the duration. The NDC hoped that Clark could succeed in tapping those same financial backers who supported the McCarthy/Kennedy movement in 1968.

In the following months, NDC followed the activities of the McGovern and O'Hara Commissions with great interest, supporting local NDC groups which presented their cases during regional Commission hearings. In the meantime, Senator Harris, as Chairman of the Democratic National Committee, appointed another investigative commission, The Freedom to Vote Task Force, chaired by Ramsey Clark, former US Attorney General. When the final version of the McGovern Report was released in November, 1969, the NDC could well be satisfied that the intent of the Convention mandate had been preserved.

The twenty-eight member Commission on Party Structure and Delegate Selection, the McGovern Commission, had been conducting hearings, reviewing state election laws and preparing a set of guidelines since its first meeting March 1, 1969. The eighteen requirements in the guidelines removed many impediments to Party participation, made delegate selection a more democratic process and guaranteed a more timely selection of delegates among other reforms. The report was published as MANDATE FOR REFORM, Report of the Commission on Party Structure and Delegate Selection to the Democratic National Committee.

27

The atmosphere of optimism generated by the McGovern Commission report however, was considerably dampened for the NDC by the cloud of financial crisis. Blair Clark resigned as treasurer in December, 1969, complaining that the Coalition had difficulty raising money. The veracity of that statement was underlined by the disclosed debt of $20,000. This was followed by the resignation of Donald M. Green who had earlier replaced Earl Craig as acting executive director. Green left the NDC to join John Kenneth Galbraith's self-styled electoral lobbying organization, Referendum '70, serving as Washington director.

The NDC appeared to be in ebb tide as this moment of its history. Many journalists were already preparing its obituary and in their coverage had demoted it to a "splinter group." Without funds, with a crumbling national organization and with an ever decreasing number of active state clubs , the NDC called a national conference in Chicago. February 13-15, 1969.

RETURN TO CHICAGO

It was appropriate that the NDC , in search of revitalization, should hold its first national convention in Chicago, the city of its conception. By returning to Chicago one and one-half years later, the Coalition refreshed those memories of inequity, abuse and violence they had suffered during the Democratic National Convention. Their return, however, was hardly triumphal. Fewer than five hundred persons, representing twenty-eight state organizations attended. The siege of Chicago had not yet opened the gates of the Democratic Party to the dissidents. But, then again, neither had the siege been lifted.

The mood at the NDC Chicago convention was one

of realism with its resultant frustrations. In the keynote address Senator Harold Hughes described the liberals' present condition as being "in disarray and somewhat dispirited." Rep. Allard Lowenstein in his address said quite bluntly while describing the NDC that "we are still in trouble as a species." In trouble was precisely where the Coalition stood. There was, expectedly, disappointment expressed by many delegates and in some cases recrimination.

This was witnessed by the underlying bitterness within the Statement of Political Purpose adopted by the convention. The document, composed by Arnold Kaufman, turned on the Democratic leaders who had long ago turned a deaf ear to the NDC; "Thus with important exceptions, the Democratic Party leaders have responded to war and racism, the two fundamental issues of our day, with business as usual. Despite the ferment of 1968, little seems to have been learned, less improved." Kaufman's statement was peppered with open threats of rebellion against the Democratic Party. If a Democratic candidate does not meet the requirements of the NDC, the Statement read, "then we will withhold support for the Democrat, perhaps even throw active support to his opponent." Speaking directly to the Party leaders, Kaufman's statement warned in unmistakeable language that the NDC "bound not by ties of party loyalty but by loyalty to values and programs," was prepared to break totally from the Party if it concluded that the Democrats were unwilling or unable to assimilate their political aims.

Most observers at the convention sensed the mood of disillusionment and crisis. Paul R. Wieck, reporting on the convention in the NEW REPUBLIC(2/28/70) recognized the symptoms and pronounced the NDC to be in "bad shape." He diagnosed the ailment as the atrophy of an organization which lacked the emotional charge and direction of a charismatic political leader. Mr. Wieck was correct in his observation, there was no charismatic leader, but he was missing the point. The reason for being of the NDC was issues not personalities. To submit to the temptation of attractive political figures would mean surrender of that potential political effectiveness, albeit unrealized at that time, which promised the realization of issue oriented goals. The NDC was an experiment in political science; a political movement without a leader. They could not be burdened with the vicissitudes or compromisability of personalities. Issues were their guiding light and attainment of common goals decided their direction.

The turmoil of Chicago in 1968 had spawned the New Democratic Coalition. Now the crisis of Chicago, 1970, was rebuilding the NDC. Seeing the danger of extinction, the gathered delegates used their opportunity to recommit themselves to the issues which had brought the Coalition into being.

NEW LEADERSHIP

A new Steering Committee was formed chaired by Marvin Madeson of Missouri, a realistic businessman with ties both in the Party and without. His strategy was to reduce the role of the national staff and return to the strength of the grass roots, encouraging and cooperating with local and national interest groups such as the National Welfare Rights Organization, The Vietnam Moratorium, the Youth Franchise Coalition, the National Committee for an Effective Congress, SANE, the Mexican American Political Association, the American Indian Movement and others. By doing this he hoped to create a tide of politically active interest groups which could rock the Democratic Party and move the dissidents toward power bringing new blood into old institutions.

The new Steering Committee held its first meeting a month after Chicago, March 14, 1970, at the Chase Park Plaza Hotel in St. Louis. Those attending included the following: Alan Baron(IA); Earl Craig(MN); Woody Duncan(KS); Rory Ellinger(MO); Al Fishman (MI); Sanford Gottlieb(DC); Joyce Harrell(SD); James Kroll(WI); Bill Lunsford(MD); Marv Madeson(MO); Mary McPartland(IO); Midge Miller(WI) ; Bob Pomeroy (KS); Frederick Ruf(CA); Caryl Steinberg(IL); Robert Toal(IN).

Madeson announced a $975.58 balance in the treasury with some bills outstanding. With that reality firmly in mind, the group discussed the possible functions of the national organization. A limited role was decided upon assigning to the national organization the responsibility of maintaining a newsletter, keeping in touch with the Democratic Congress, assisting states in developing local organizations and perhaps establishing a speakers and entertainers bureau to support local fund raising.

Madeson, convinced that the NDC must remain an issues organization, not a candidate-oriented group, introduced a resolution which prevented those who were "candidates for public office, public office holders or closely associated with any candidate," from becoming NDC officers. Five vice-chairmen were then selected: John Cashin of Alabama, Midge Miller of Wisconsin, Dick Noble of Michigan, Sonia Sloan of Deleware and I. Philip Sipser of New York.

To establish communication among the decentralized state NDC organizations, Joyce Harrell, the NDC secretary from South Dakota, was selected to begin publication of a national newsletter. Woody Duncan of Kansas and Peter Donhowe of Missouri were asked to assist in the newsletter project which, it was estimated, would cost $3000 per hundred thousand copies. It was a major expenditure for the financially weak organization but one which was essential to the maintainance of a national structure.

A major revamping of the Coalition's national organization also occurred at this Steering Committee meeting. As directed by the Chicago convention, the committee members created a national structure based on five geographical regions: Northeast, Southeast, Central, Rocky and Far West. Each region was to elect a chairman. In the interim, the regional directors were appointed by the national chairman. Bill Lundsford was named regional director of the Northeast; Bob Pomeroy, regional director of the Central; and three other directors for the remaining regions were to be named by Madeson at a later time.

The actualize the NDC doctrine of creating political activists to work in a grass-roots capacity, the March Steering Committee meeting approved the establishment of an NDC Intern Program headed by Alan Baron of Iowa. The idea proved to be an excellent one. Meeting in Washington, D.C. the following June, 1970, the Interns gained important knowledge in campaign planning, volunteer recruiting, polling, fund raising, canvassing, etc. This knowledge was used immediately in the '70 elections to help reelect Senators Hartke, Burdick and Montoya and others for whom the Interns worked.

The next Steering Committee meeting was held in the home of Mr. and Mrs. Ferris Owen in Chevy Chase, Maryland, June 12-14, 1970. It was a low keyed gathering, discussing organizationally important

32

issues on a limited agenda: utilization of student activists, political workshop training, communications, making NDC more effective and financing. The heavy and confusing rhetoric of earlier meetings was absent. Consensus was reached on several issues: (1) the NDC should lead a long range program on Party reform titled "An Open Party as a Vehicle For Change, " (2) the national newsletter should continue, (3) other political intern programs should follow the June training session, and (4) NDC should continue to act as a coordinating body for state organizations.

The Steering Committee had matured considerably since those early free-wheeling and boisterous meetings. Marvin Madeson, though having little more than a skeleton organization with which to work, was handling his task in a businesslike and effective manner.

In the meantime, primary elections were taking place and candidates were pressing their campaigns on toward November. Support of individual candidates was the responsibility of state NDC organizations. The New York NDC, one of the stronger state groups, held a statewide convention in New York City February 28, 1970. Four hundred delegates gathered, claiming representation of 25,000 members, to endorse candidates for state and national offices. Their choice for US Senator from a field of Democrats including Richard Ottinger, Ben Rosenthal and Richard McCarthy was Paul O'Dwyer, a founder of NDC. Other endorsed candidates were Basil Patterson, the Harlem politician, for Lt. Governor; Adam Walinsky, ex-aide to Kennedy, for the post of Attorney General; and for Governor, Eugene Nickerson, former Nassau County Executive.

Other state NDC groups or affiliates had important stakes in the primaries and elections of 1970. In Ohio there was John Gilligan for Governor, Ralph Yarborough for Senator in Texas, Frank Moss for Senator in Utah,

Joe Duffy for Senator in Connecticut, Phillip Hoff for Senator in Vermont, Chicago Alderman A.A. (Sammy) Rayner for Congressman in Illinois, Don Peterson and Pat Lucey running against one another in the Wisconsin gubernatorial primary, and others.

As the state organizations threw themselves into the thicket of local political affairs and campaigns, the national NDC continued its search for Party reform. In an October '70 activity letter, Marv Madeson reported that an NDC task force composed of Arnie Weiss, Ken Bode, Verne Newton and others was observing and lobbying the O'Hara Rules Commission. Madeson and others had written the O'Hara Commission explaining the NDC position and reiterating their devotion to Party reform. In meeting personally with members of the O'Hara Commission in Washington, D.C., the NDC task force was able to convey its opinions and contribute information in addition to guarding against neglect of the '68 Convention's mandate.

Although the McGovern Commission guidelines had already been completed, they were far from total implementation at that time. The NDC had sent one hundred fund raising letters to garner support for the implementation of the guidelines. By October, Madeson was able to announce the receipt of over seven hundred dollars. Meanwhile the NDC, through the efforts of Madeson and Sandy Gottlieb, placed a support-seeking ad in the November 7, 1970, issue of the NEW REPUBLIC. Other avenues of support for Party reform were also being sought.

NATIONAL REFORM

Finally, in the early part of 1971, the NDC was able
to reap the seed of reform which it had been sowing
since those lean days in 1968. In January the O'Hara
Commission met and approved a final version of their
recommendations calling for a greatly reformed alloca-
tion of state Convention votes. The Commission formula apportioned delegates to the Convention on the basis
of two equally considered factors - state population and
the state Democratic Presidential votes in the 1960,
1964 and 1968 elections. The recommendations broke
from the precedent of using a state's electoral college
strength as an apportionment factor. Instead, they ad-
hered to the recently developed one-man-one-vote concept, a form of purer democracy which had been taking
shape in the decisions of the US Judiciary since the major Supreme Court decision in BAKER V. CARR(1962).
　The Executive Committee of the Democratic National
Committee, meeting February 17, 1971, in Washington,
D.C., was unwilling to accept such drastic reform as
embodied in the O'Hara Commission report. Instead
it substituted its own recommendations which called
for delegate apportionment based on (1) the average
Democratic vote in Presidential elections during 1960,
1964 and 1968 and (2) the electoral college strength of
each state - three convention votes per elector. The
Executive Committee formula would allocate 47% of

35

the delegate votes based on Democratic strength and
53% based on electoral college strength. Although the
actual numbers difference between the two porposals
was not considerable, in ideology they were far apart.
What the O'Hara Commission had done was to adapt
the one-man-one-vote doctrine which had already been
applied to electoral bodies from state legislatures to
school boards, to the party convention system. The
Executive Committee was unwilling to accept the im-
plications of such a change. They prefered to retain
at least the semblance of small state power even though
it meant disproportionate representation.

The Executive Committee did, however, accept
uncompromised the McGovern Commission recommendations and also the O'Hara Rules Commission recommendations on procedures for conducting credential
challenge hearings at the national Convention. The
procedural guidelines for credential challenges required
the early filing of challenge documents naming the
grounds for the challenge and allowing the challenged
a right of rebuttal. It provided for open hearings conducted by a "person who is known by reputation to be
fair and impartial in the context of the challenge and
is experienced in the law, particularly in fact finding
and procedural due process." And it established guar-
antees for impartial consideration of challenges by the
Credentials Committee including the requirement that
all Committee members receive copies of the Committee report prior to the start of the Convention. The inclusion of these provisions was a considerable victory
for men such as Stephen Mitchell, a member of the
O'Hara Rules Commission, who had experienced the
inequities of the '68 Convention hearings.

The full Democratic National Committee, meeting
two days later, February 19, 1971, considered a total
of seven proposed apportionment formulas including

the uncompromised O'Hara Commission plan and the
Executive Committee's plan. The full Committee
accepted the Executive Committee's plan. They also
accepted the Executive Committee's approval of the
McGovern Commission recommendations and the
O'Hara Commission procedural guidelines for credential challenges. However, in an unexpected vote, the
DNC accepted Committeeman John E. Power's motion
to permit national committeemen seating at the '72
Convention. It had earlier been generally accepted
that the provision of the Convention Call requiring
"timely" selection of the delegates would prevent the
committeemen, most of whom were elected in 1968,
from gaining Convention voting privileges. The stage
appeared to be set for a challenge of all Democratic
National Committee members at the 1972 Convention.

Many of the Party reforms that NDC and others
had argued for since Chicago, were now sanctioned
by the Party's chief organ and incorporated within
the Call for the 1972 Convention. Yet the affair was
far from ended. Thirteen reform minded activists,
dissatisfied with the National Committee's rejection
of the O'Hara Commission apportionment formula,
took their case to the Federal Judiciary. A law suit,
filed March 15, 1971, in the US District Court of
Washington, D.C., named the Democratic Party, the
Democratic National Committee, National Committee
Chairman Lawrence O'Brien and Treasurer Robert
S. Strauss as defendants in an action requesting the
court to (1) declare the DNC-adopted apportionment
formula unconstitutional, (2) enjoin the Democratic
Party from using that formula at the 1972 Convention,
and (3) declare as a proper formula one which is
"based upon the number of Democratic voters voting
in one or more immediately proceeding Presidential

elections." The thirteen plantiffs included large state party officials such as John English of New York and Rep. Shirley Chisholm also of New York and others such as Joseph Duffey, Chairman of the Americans For Democratic Action (ADA) and Kenneth Bode, Director of the Center for Political Reform and formerly Research Director of the McGovern Commission.

Their complaint stated that the DNC's apportionment formula and the inclusion of the DNC members in the Convention, discriminated against large states in favor of small ones. The one-man-one-vote doctrine was the foundation of their contention as stated in the complaint:

In developing the one-man-one-vote rationale in a variety of closely analogous situations, the Supreme Court has held that malapportionment occurs when there is a dilution of votes. Accordingly, apportionment of a representative body must be based upon the number of actual voters represented; the one-man-one-vote doctrine is based on the concept of one "relevant man" and for the purposes of the Democratic Party and its nominating convention, the only relevant man is a Democrat.

The District Court upheld the challengers but that decision was reversed by the Circuit Court of Appeals.

Meanwhile, the NDC national organization continued to serve as a coordinating body for local reform movements. National approval of the McGovern and O'Hara reforms was one thing, actual state implementation of those reforms was another. It was up to NDC groups across the country to rally reform elements around the Party reform resolutions forcing needed enabling legislation through state legislatures.

The national NDC organization remained unfunded

and unstable as was demonstrated by the forced cancellation of a planned national meeting April 3, 1971 in St. Louis. But there was still a real grass-roots movement composed of minority groups, reform advocates and Party dissidents. To these people NDC was a symbol of their movement and a reminder that they were not alone in their fight to reform the Party. Conceived in the inequities of the Chicago Convention and tempered by continual crisis, the NDC proved effective in promoting change and equally important, in demonstrating the strength of liberal-reform politics in America. As those who had remained loyal to the NDC ideal since the Battle of Chicago scattered to support various candidates and campaigns in 1972, they did so with the knowledge that at last they had a chance to win.

WE WERE

THE DEMOCRATIC PARTY

IN EXILE

MY NDC INITIATION

When I was introduced to the New Democratic Coalition of Rhode Island my potential political energy was running high. Like all NEW YORK TIMES readers, I was opposed to the War, appalled by the carnage displayed on Huntley-Brinkley and disgusted with Johnson's lies, bumbling and down-home stupidity. I had been fired up by the poetry and glamour of the McCarthy and Kennedy campaigns and tried by the emotion wrenching, enraging tragedies of Bobby's death and Gene's defeat. With my television eyes I had seen the scandal of Chicago's Finest cracking open the skull of my generation in front of the Conrad Hilton.

And I was moved by personal experience - a high school friend coming home for Christmas, his leg blasted off by a misplaced mine and others who never returned. I had gone to Washington, D.C. for the 1968 Peace March protesting with a half-million others in the cold marble capital to stone deaf leaders. And again in 1969 I was in DC for the Counter-inaugural Ball, a spine-straightening, songful demonstration highlighted for me by Phil Ochs belting out in Dylan-style under a big-top tent jammed with high spirited protestors his anti-War song I DECLARE THE WAR IS OVER. I took that message back to Brown University with me forming yet another anti-War group which I called I Declare the War Is Over Committee. Every now and then I set up a table in the Post Office lobby manned by a couple friends. Armed with a stack of telegram forms we urged students to spend a buck and send their anti-War message to President Nixon. Western Union was more than grateful for the business.

AT BROWN UNIVERSITY

During the last semester of my senior year at Brown, the first months of 1971, I had signed up for an independent studies project, one sponsored by the political science department but thoroughly the creation of the NDC. The topic for the study group was electoral reform. Most of the students in the project had been associated with NDC in the past and saw this as a convenient way to get course credit for their otherwise extra-curricular political activities. I just stumbled into it seeing a loosely defined project like this as a pleasant way to coast through my final term.

A Pembroke junior, Sydney Hanlon, was the uncontested leader of the group. She was a short-fused stick of distaff dynamite. I immediately recognized Syd as a force to be reckoned with. She was a small girl, only about five feet tall, with a cute, pugnosed face, wiry auburn hair and a well-proportioned, sexy body. Someone once described her as a girl with a will of her own. I'd go even further and say that once Syd had set her sights on something, the only wise thing to do was to step aside. At twenty she was a political dynamo with the wile of Mata Hari, the adamancy of Winston Churchill and the morals of Machiavelli. It was these three traits that carried her from the flooded ranks of stamp-licking McCarthy campaign workers in 1968 to a seat on the important Credentials Committee at the Democratic National Convention at Miami in 1972.

44

Another junior, Andy Howard, acted as unofficial vice-chairman of the study group. "Syd and Andy" was a phrase that I quickly welded into a single word like salt-and-pepper, Mutt-and-Jeff. Syd and Andy were the core of the NDC at Brown. They had both been on the summer staff. When others came and went, Syd and Andy continued working - canvassing, lobbying, sorting, telephoning. Personality-wise, Syd was the north pole and Andy the south. Although he worked hard at politics, Andy was incapable of an ulterior motive. Shy yet straightforward when pressed, if ever Andy harbored ambitions he kept them well concealed. He always wore the same baggy green work pants, matching work shirt and half-laced, scuffed work shoes. I found Andy an extremely likable person, yet there was a certain sadness about him. His pale, full moon face was always so serious. Like a lost kid he worked at the political activities without excitement or conviction. Majoring in Eastern religions and reading books like THE AUTOBIOGRAPHY OF LENNY BRUCE, Andy was an unlikely politico.

The study group fulfilled my expectations and was a pleasant punt, although we did succeed in getting some interesting research facts together which Syd worked overtime to type. The report, "Primary Election Laws: the Fifty States," was published the next year by NDC in a nicely done pamphlet with a two hundred dollar grant from Common Cause, John Gardner's electorate protection agency. Although we had the temerity to put a $1.65 price on the cover, to the best of my knowledge not more than a dozen from the two hundred edition ever sold. For me the study group was an introduction to the New Democratic Coalition of Rhode Island, which by the summer, had placed me in the nucleus of the organization. The nucleus at that time consisted of three individuals - Syd

and Andy and John Nelson, three work dogs who gave
a lion's roar to a political organization that,if statis-
tics can be trusted, didn't even exist.

225 ORMS STREET

March 3
    It was early March before I finally settled back
into the academic grind and got busy researching our
group study topic. I had found a few books on electoral reform at the library. Andy informed me that
John Nelson had quite a few others at the NDC office.
He called John who invited us over.
    The NDC office and John's apartment - one in the
same- was located in a working-class, white man's
ghetto. Several years before, the concrete and
steel of the Boston to New York expressway had sev-
ered it from the heart of Providence, but it remained
within view of the capitol dome. Nelson rented the
top floor of a three-story row house on Orms Street.
It was as featureless as all the other houses on Orms
Street and enclosed by a waist-high, chain-link fence
that kept Toothless Tony's yapping mongrel in and the
sidewalk out.
    Andy pressed the back door buzzer. After a while,
the landlord, Tony, stuck his head out a first floor
window, "It's busted. Don't waste yah time. But I
seen John come in an hour ago and I ain't seen him
leave yet so just go on up. Don't make no difference."
He told us to be sure to close the door, too, because,
as he explained it with intermittent whistling caused
by the air rushing past two bicuspid vacancies, he
wasn't heating the whole neighborhood.
    The narrow, spiraling staircase leading to the
third floor was as steep and dark as a castle watch-

tower. On the second floor landing we were inundated
with the warm and spicy pasta smells of an Italian
family's dinner. Andy said the family was constantly
arguing and always in Italian. At the top of the stairs
we knocked on Nelson's apartment door.

John came to the door wearing a pair of brown
corduroy slacks and an undershirt. He greeted us
with an enthusiastic "Hi, good," and a wide smile.
"I didn't hear the buzzer."

"No, you wouldn't have,"Andy said. "It's 'busted.'"

"Good. Come on in." John was a lanky twenty-
six year old looking a bit underfed, but with bright,
sometimes sparkling blue eyes, a finely featured face
and carefully trimmed blondish brown hair. From
appearances he could have been an innovative young
architect or a computer analyst. He left Andy and
me in the kitchen while he went into the bedroom to
put on a shirt.

There were several mismatched lunch plates
on the table and a rice-crusted frying pan on the stove.
I peaked into the small living room. It was sparsely
furnished - a tattered green sofa, splintered coffee
table, threadbare rug and, in the corner, someones
discarded dining room table which was cluttered with
papers, envelopes, pamphlets, file cards and a long-
corded black telephone. A black cat sat placidly on
the green sofa toying with a dangling shred of uphol-
stery.

"Come on Pooh Bear, you know better than that."
John swatted at the cat as he crossed the living room.
He led us back across the stairway hall into a small,
adjacent room that served as his office. Along three
walls unstained plywood boards on two-by-four legs
provided considerable desk space. Jerrybuilt wooden
bookshelves sagged from mounds of books, pamphlets
and newspapers. An antiquated Underwood typewriter

rested in a corner. Bright silk-screen posters covered cracks in the plaster walls. One poster in bold red lettering read "Arcaro For State Senator." Another in cobalt blue read "Open Primary." A bare, hundred watt bulb dangled on a long frayed wire from the center of the ceiling.

John said he had quite a few books that might be helpful to the study project. Rummaging through a closet he pulled out one after the other: The Democratic Choice, A Report of the Commission on the Democratic Selection of Presidential Nominees, Harold Hughes, Chairman; Proposal For Direct Presidential Primary System by Joseph Gebhardt; Report of the Election Law Study Commission of the State of Rhode Island, 1957. He continued to pile books on the counter: Minority Report of the Election Law Study; Legislative Supplement to the Report of Election Law Study; Resume of the Delegate Selection Reform by the Democratic Party of Rhode Island Since the Chicago Convention; The Rhode Island Democratic Party 1956-66, From Unity to Disunity; Campaign Manual: Rhode Island Democratic Committee Seminar; Politics, Parties and Pressure Groups.

"Maybe you could sort through some of this stuff too." He dragged out two cardboard boxes stuffed with notes, photographs, campaign literature, flyers and some "Clean Gene" decals. Talking excitedly as if he had just stumbled upon some attic relic of his better days, John told us he had kept meticulous notes of the McCarthy campaign in Rhode Island always planning to write that story as the history of a grassroots movement. "And here's another unfinished project." He pulled out another box of papers and pamphlets. "This was supposed to be a new type of high school civics book." He explained that a girl who had worked on the McCarthy campaign had collected this material with plans to organize a "revolutionary" high school text. "But after the campaign she got busy with other things and faded."

In all, John had given me about twenty books; eighteen more than I felt I really wanted. The day before I had run across a new book on politics titled SMOKE FILLED ROOMS. I asked John if he had read that yet. "No. I haven't had time to read any books lately," he replied. I noticed then that the books stacked in my arms were very dusty.

We talked for awhile. With some probing, John began talking about himself and how he had gotten involved in Rhode Island politics. As with many students, it was the War that led him into politics. John had been a biology major at Brown. He had worked with another Brown student on a pamphlet called "Brown Student Leaders Speak Out on Vietnam." John came down with mononucleosis that year and had to return the next to complete his senior year courses. Anti-War fever was running high on college campuses then. An obscure senator from Minnesota had picked up the colors early and before long had rallied an army of student workers.

John, more articulate and informed than most, literally found himself a spokesman for the movement, satisfying the younger students' craving for facts. He described one incident to us that he saw as a milestone in his turn toward politics. He had attended a Hubert Humphrey meeting at the Biltmore Hotel in Providence. Unexpectedly, he met some state Democratic leaders on the elevator, talking with them as they rode down, about the history of US involvement in Vietnam. They were interested and receptive to the topic, even pressing John for more information. With a new found optimism, John doubled his efforts. Then the bottom dropped out of the movement; Kennedy's assassination, McCarthy's final defeat and ultimately, the election of Richard Nixon.

49

All that could be done after the election was for
the old protestors to reunite and recommit themselves
to change which they did in forming the New Democratic Coalition. John said that the first days of the NDC
in Rhode Island went slowly. Its first chairman, John
Walsh, "did little if any work, never returned phone
calls and refused to let others follow through with programs." Consequently, John said, "There was alot
of maneuvering in the early stages of NDC to eliminate some of the goldbrickers." It was not until the
Moratorium Day protest in October, 1969, that the
NDC began to solidify. Walsh finally left and was
replaced by James Fugere, a more realistic administrator. Nelson had largely assumed managing res-
ponsibilities at this time, leading the NDC through
the resparked protests, demonstrations and student
strikes. NDC lent support to select candidates in the
1970 state election including the winner of the gubernatorial race, Frank Licht, and an important state
senator, Harold Arcaro. Chairman Fugere quit at
this point to take a job with the Licht administration.
Jack Indeck, the vice-chairman, moved up a notch,
"a little reluctantly," as John put it.

I asked John why he hadn't been offered a job with
the Licht administration. By his own description,
Nelson had worked hard at the campaign and was probably as entitled to the spoils of victory as much as anyone. He surprised me by saying he had been offered
a job on the Governor's staff and at a respectable salary; but he had decided that working from the outside
would be more effective, so he declined. I remember
thinking when he said this that it was a ridiculously
noble position to take. As the course of events proved,
however, he was correct in assuming he would be more
effective in attaining NDC goals from the outside. But
since graduating, John had lived as a pauper; teaching

for a year at a Providence high school then leaving that to devote more time to NDC, driving a cab at night to pay for room and board. Even George Washington might have made some concessions for a moments reprieve from Valley Forge.

John, during those days, was really waging a one man campaign against the system. The Rhode Island NDC was hardly generating enough income to feed him and there was still printing costs and advertising fees. Its membership roll, even though a bare one hundred or so names, was still nothing more than a list; it might just as well have been torn from last year's telephone directory. But John was determined to change the system that had created and perpetuated the War. He saw electoral reform as the only way to do it and NDC as the best available tool. So he put his back into it working on a project level, one step at a time. With the help of other reform-minded Democrats he had drawn up and presented to the Rhode Island legislature a Presidential primary reform bill. That was the current NDC project.

Andy and I talked with John about the primary bill for another hour. It was dark before we left John's apartment, made our way down the winding staircase, past Toothless Tony's yapping mongrel, out the gate and eventually back to the well-lighted streets of Brown University.

ELECTORAL REFORM

1969

    After the debacle of the '68 Chicago Convention,
the national Democratic leaders knew that the time
for change had arrived. They were making studied
movements in that direction soon after Humphrey's
November defeat. The first move was to appoint
Senator George McGovern chairman of the Commission on Party Structure and Delegate Selection.
McGovern quickly organized a staff and began an am-
bitious series of sixteen hearings across the country.
Rhode Island's turn to testify came on July 10, 1969,
in Boston.

    Six months earlier in preparation for these re-
gional meetings, the Democratic National Committee
Chairman, Senator Fred Harris, had sent a letter to
each state party chairman requesting that they form
a local task force to prepare evidence to be presented
at the hearings. In Rhode Island, Harris' letter was
politely filed and ignored, first by Governor Licht's
new state party chairman, Anthony Giannini, then,
after he was appointed to a judgeship, by his replacement, state representative John Hogan. Undeterred,
Nelson and the NDC formed their own task force, the
Hargrove Commission, under the chairmanship of a
Brown University political science professor.

    John Nelson and Jim Fugere were at the Boston
hearing to present the NDC's research findings as
was state party chairman John Hogan to defend his
position. Fugere rose to present the findings of the
Hargrove Commission. He commended Governor
Licht's Presidential preference primary law enacted
at the most recent General Assembly session, as a
step in the right direction; "But it doesn't go nearly

far enough. It's done nothing to increase accessability to the state's delegate selection process. It leaves unresolved many problems involved in selecting a representative delegation reflective of the will of all party voters. In Rhode Island we need to extend the end of the January deadline for Presidential candidates to declare themselves in order to be on the ballot. As it stands now, both Senator Robert Kennedy and Vice-President Hubert Humphrey would have been excluded in last year's voting rendering the preference poll senseless.

"And we also need to abolish the twenty-six month rule which prevents a voter from crossing party lines for that length of time after participating in an earlier primary. Unless we enact these changes and soon, the Rhode Island delegation may be refused seating at the 1972 Convention."

John Hogan took a considerably different attitude toward the state election laws: "We in Rhode Island have done a pretty fair job in responding to the call for liberalizing. There's been no disregard of reform since I've been chairman. I'm totally in agreement with the idea of party reform, but I'm not in agreement with change for the sake of change, or changes for which I don't have a sensible reason." In a thinly veiled reference to Nelson, "You don't jump in and change everything. You get your feet on the ground and find out where you're going . . . the older people in the party are naturally a little bit slow to accept change, so I've tried to respect both sides; the reformists and the old people."

Nelson was a great political strategist. Like a good chess player he played his moves three turns in advance. He knew that Harris' letter calling for a state task force on reform had been ignored. Hogan wanted to forget about it. A month before the Boston McGovern Com-

mission meeting the NDC refreshed his memory. The
PROVIDENCE EVENING BULLETIN article(6/3/69)
titled "Coalition Seeks Task Force" read: "The NDC
of Rhode Island today called upon Rep. John Hogan,
the new Democratic state chairman, to name a task
force for reforming state party procedures in con-
junction with a similar national effort.

"James E. Fugere, chairman of the coalition. . .
wrote Mr. Hogan that 'changes in the Democratic
Party are necessary to its survival. . . '. The coalition letter said a predecessor as chairman, Judge
Anthony A. Giannini, had been asked in March to form,
the task force but none had resulted. "

Then the day before the Boston hearing, Fugere
met with Hogan to, as Nelson stated it in an intra-
Coalition memo, "extract from him a committment
to form a task force. The state chairman evidenced
not the slightest interest, having his hands full with
internal party problems - foremost, in acting as a
buffer in a patronage feud between the Governor and
the Providence City Committee Chairman Larry
McGarry - and said he would make no such announcement. "

Now, at the Boston hearing, Hogan was set up.
Standing before a commission of reform-devoted national Party regulars, having been publically reminded
of his failure to act on the task force request and having
just testified that he was all in favor of party reform.
Nelson quickly scribbled something onto a piece of
paper and passed it over to McGovern's specially appointed Commission advisor, Mrs. Ann Wexler of the
Connecticut NDC. Mrs. Wexler read the note then
looked back to Hogan and asked, "Mr. Hogan, as you
know, several months ago the Democratic National
Chairman sent a letter to each state chairman requesting

54

that they form local task forces to investigate party reform. How has Rhode Island responded to this request?"

Snared! Hogan considered his alternatives for a moment then said that certainly he had plans for such a task force and would pursue them. An article in the next days EVENING BULLETIN(6/11/69) titled "Move on Reform Pleases Coalition Leader," read: "The chairman of the NDC of Rhode Island today congratulated the Democratic state chairman for agreeing to establish a state task force on party reform. The congratulations were extended to Rep. John J. Hogan of Cumberland by James E. Fugere. Mr. Hogan said yesterday in Boston . . . that the task force would be created.

"Mr. Fugere . . . said Mr. Hogan's announcement convinces him 'that our mutual resolve to make an even more open and responsive Democratic Party will result in the healthiest Democratic Party possible.' "

Nelson was playing his hand well. Hogan, however, was no political dummy. The McGovern Commission was just so much reformist hullabaloo in 1969 and could be easily ignored, which Hogan did. That changed, however, when the Democratic National Committee officially incorporated the Commission Guidelines into the Call to the 1972 Convention.

1970

I don't know how NDC got a copy of this letter, but they did and printed up a few hundred copies to be sure the message got out. The letter from the Commission on Party Structure and Delegate Selection was addressed to the Honorable John J. Hogan, Chairman of the Democratic State Committee of Rhode Island and dated February 27, 1970.

The letter read as follows:

Dear Mr. Hogan:

In December 1969, we sent you a copy of the Official Guidelines for Delegate Selection of the Commission on Party Structure and Delegate Selection. In keeping with the Commission's obligation to aid the states in meeting the requirements of the Call to the 1972 Convention, the Commission staff has analyzed the delegate selection process in your state as it relates to the Guidelines.

The enclosed analysis is based on the best information available to the Commission at this time. For each state, we have compiled and evaluated the election laws, Democratic Party rules and practices, testimony taken at our public hearings, statements submitted to our offices, and newspaper accounts of the delegate selection process. If your understanding of the process in your state differs from the analysis, we hope you will contact us at your earliest convenience.

The analysis is limited to: (1) those laws, rules, and practices in your state that are inconsistant with the mandatory requirements of the Commission Guidelines; and (2) those Guidelines that the Commission urges state Parties to adopt.

In most cases, conformity with the Guidelines - a copy of which is attached for your ready reference - can be achieved in several ways. We are prepared to offer you whatever technical assistance you may need to evaluate and respond to the analysis. You will note that we specifically deal with the following Guidelines for the state of Rhode Island: A-2, A-5, B-4, C-4.

Since the beginning of Commission deliberations, we have been encouraged by the commitment to reform demonstrated by Party leaders. We believe that the

adoption of the Commission's Guidelines, along with
local reform efforts, will ensure a strong and winning
Democratic Party.

Sincerely yours,

George McGovern

Enclosures
cc: Hon. Joseph A. Doorley, Jr.
    Mrs. Isabel Leeds

Still the state party regulars sat on the issue,
waiting to see just how seriously all this reform talk
was being taken. Meanwhile, Nelson was moving fast
as ever, not leaving a single stone unturned.   At
Faneuil Hall in Boston on May 15, 1970, he testified
before a regional meeting of the Rules Committee of
the Democratic National Committee:

"The testimony I will give this morning will be nearly
identical to that which we gave to the McGovern Commission on July 10, 1969, for the simple reason that
the Democratic Party of Rhode Island has done nothing
about recommendations in that testimony.
"Last July we reiterated before the McGovern Commission our plea that the state chairman of Rhode
Island appoint a task force to study Rhode Island's
problems of party reform in cooperation with the
Commission, as he had been asked to do by Fred
Harris on January 17, 1969. Mr. Hogan, although
he stated before the Commission his intention to form
such a task force, has still made no effort whatsoever
to do so.
"I would suggest that it is the responsibility of the

Democratic National Committee to persuade state parties to study their own problems and to advise those
parties when they are out of compliance with recommendations to be officially proposed by the McGovern
Commission in 1972 for acceptance by the Convention.
I would hope that your Rules Committee would have
a role in the enforcement of this responsibility.

"As it stands now, the McGovern Commission is
headed in one direction while the Democratic Party
of Rhode Island is going another. This is definately
a collision course, because when they both come together at the Convention, there will be a crunch that
will again rip the Democratic Party wide open.

"To cite one example, I would like to compare the
courses of the Rhode Island party and the McGovern
Commission on the matter of delegate selection.

"By applying the new Presidential primary as introduced and passed by the Democratic party last year,
I think it will become apparent that the primary leaves
the delegate selection process of 1968 essentially unchanged. Let's apply that Presidential primary to the
situation of the 1968 campaign and see how well it functions.

"When you walked into a voting booth in March, 1968,
you would have faced three columns. The first two
regard the selection of people you would like to see go
to the Convention, the last column is for the preference
poll. Let's look at the last column first.

"For the sake of argument, let's say that you could
have voted for any candidate whether or not he had
announced (of course, at the time of the primary, the
second Tuesday in March, only McCarthy had announced, and Johnson had been drafted in New Hampshire.) So you would have voted for McCarthy, Johnson
or Kennedy. Then comes the time of the Convention
in August, and - oops, Kennedy's dead, Johnson's with-

drawn, Humphrey's emerged, McGovern stands in, and McCarthy is the only one of the orinnals left in the running. It is hard to imagine that the preference poll taken in March would mirror public preference, and therefore have any validity, in August. And even if it did, the delegates selected to go to the Convention are in no way bound to the poll by the primary law. So you may as well not pull the third column levers at all. In fact, you may as well save the public's money and erase it from the ballot.

"The second column is for pledged delegate candidates, all pledged candidates in March of 1968 would have been for McCarthy. Of course there couldn't have been any pledged McCarthy candidates in March because the kids hadn't gotten back from New Hampshire to begin to build the McCarthy organization. Even if there had been, no one would have voted for them in March because it was never believed that McCarthy would knock Johnson out, everyone was waiting to see whether Kennedy would announce, and, in short, no voter could have been sure enough of how the race would unfold to have the confidence of judgement necessary to vote for a pledged candidate. So you may as well not pull those levers either and erase the second column from the ballot too.

"That leaves the first column. Applying the state primary laws, the first slate on the ballot would be the endorsed Democratic slate with an asterisk next to every slot and headed by figures known statewide - Pastore, Pell, Licht and others. Slates for other candidates not endorsed by the Democratic Party of Rhode Island would be strewn across the ballot according to alphabetical order.

"So we are right back where we were in 1968, with party endorsement being the only viable mechanism for delegate selection and with an unpledged delegation going unbound to the Convention. The only reason I can think of which could rationalize this Presidential primary, is the hope by party officials to circumvent the 'timeliness rule' of the Convention.

"Now, the McGovern recommendations state: 'The Commission is aware that it has no authority to eliminate committee systems in their entirety. However, the Commission can and does require State Parties which elect delegates in this manner to make it clear to voters at the time the Party committee is elected or appointed that one of its functions will be the selection of National Convention delegates.'

"It is clear that unless the Democratic Party of Rhode Island makes clear to the voters of Rhode Island that the State Committee members who will be elected on September 15, 1970, will in fact select the delegation to the national Convention, it will be out of compliance with the above reccomendation.

"It is also clear that the Democratic Party of Rhode Island has no intention to alert voters to facts of party operation. There are three copies of the party by-laws that I know of; headquarters has told me for months that they are being rewritten and that no, I can't have a Xerox copy.

"The McGovern Commission report clearly provides remedies for these wrongs, but unless the states are awakened to them by the Democratic National Committee, there will be another Chicago nightmare.

"I would hope that the Rules Committee would lend its fullest support to the Commission's recommendations and communicate that support to the state parties."

60

1971

S-272

INTRODUCED BY:
Senators Harold Arcaro and Matthew Callaghan
ORDERED PRINTED BY:
Senate
REFERRED TO:
Senate Committee on Judiciary
DATE PRINTED:
February 11, 1971

STATE OF RHODE ISLAND
AND PROVIDENCE PLANTATIONS

JANUARY SESSION, A.D. 1971

AN ACT Providing For Open Presidential Primaries,
and in Amendment of Chapter 17-12.1 of the General
Laws, Entitled "Primaries for Election of Delegates
to National Conventions and for Presidential Preference "

John Gardner of Common Cause called the NDC
Open Primary Bill "a model for all states to follow."
It was a beautiful piece of legislation, a tribute to the
NDC grass-roots reform effort. However, it was never
enacted. Had it been, there would have been considerable change in the state's primary system.
Firstly, and foremost, the elected Convention delegates would have been bound to vote according to the
results of the Presidential preference poll. Secondly,
they would have been bound to vote in direct proportion to each candidate's tally. In other words, if
Muskie had received 40% of the Democratic preference
poll vote and Humphrey 60%, Muskie would have been

61

assured 40% of the state's Convention votes. In 1968 McCarthy outpolled Humphrey in a popularity poll yet he only received two and one-half of the state's twenty-seven Convention votes. Thirdly, the delegate candidates would be clearly identified on the ballot as pledged to one or another Presidential candidate or as uncommitted if that was the case. The party endorsed delegate candidates would no longer receive preferred first column positioning on the ballot or asterisk identification. Equality in positioning would be guaranteed by requiring that the candidates' names be rotated, that is, moved to different positions on the ballot as different groups of ballots were printed, and then the ballots would be distributed to polling places in a random fashion.

Fourthly, the bill would have moved the primary date back from April 11 to June 12 to make the results "timely" in relation to the Convention date. Fifthly, it would have eliminated the twenty-six month rule which forbid voters from crossing party lines after having voted in a primary within that period. And lastly, in the Open Primary, the delegates would have to run within Congressional districts, not statewide.

This bill, prepared and drafted by the New Democratic Coalition of Rhode Island, was introduced on the state Senate floor by Senators Harold C. Arcaro, Jr. and Matthew F. Callaghan, Jr., both "liberal" Providence Democrats. I put "liberal" within quotation marks to qualify the term. It's an adjective not often found in front of the phrase "Providence Democrats." Arcaro and Callaghan were no political ingenues. They understood and worked within the party machine. But they were young, a little rebellious and not as afraid of change as their seniors. They agreed to present the bill but everyone knew that it was up to John Nelson to follow through.

LOBBYING

March 4

It was my turn to lobby for S-272 on the Senate
floor. John, Syd and Andy had rounded up twenty-six
students and NDC members to lobby for the bill. For
the first couple weeks there was alot of interest and
enthusiasm - it was no problem scheduling two or
three to come to the State House during each day's
session. Each lobbyist was given a handout sheet
with a summary of the bill, instructions on which
senators to talk to and how best to approach each one.

I arrived at the State House a half-hour before
the afternoon session was to begin. Following the
instruction sheet I first went to the Secretary of State's
office next door to the Senate chamber and registered
as a lobbyist by signing a large leather encased ledger.
The gray-haired clerk watched me print NDC in the
column after my name. "Good God, not another one.
You'll soon have more lobbyists than there are senators.
Well, good luck then," he smiled.

Most of the senators hadn't entered the Senate
chambers when I stepped in. There were only a few
huddled in finger-jabbing conversation and a couple
others at their desks writing. I had a seating chart
to identify the target senators, but the way the desks
curved around the podium made it difficult to count
the seats from the end. I walked up to a couple desks
in the middle of the chamber to read the name plate
fastened to the front. The uniformed guard who had
been eyeing me closely since I entered, left his door-
side post and beelined to me.

"You must be with the press?" he asked suspiciously. I had pulled my Brooks Brothers three-piece
tweed suit out of moth balls for this occasion, shined

my wingtips and even slicked down my long, frizzy
hair; but I apparently looked no more respectable than
a reporter.
 "No, no," I stumbled. "I'm a lobbyist for the NDC."
 "For what?"
 "The New Democratic Coaltion," I enunciated.
 "What does the 'N' stand for? National?" He was
looking me over very carefully.
 "No, 'New' although we are national too."
 "And you do this for a living, do you?"
 "No, I'm a student at Brown."
 "Oh, Brown is it? Well, I understand now." He
suddenly seemed satisfied. "I saw that rucksack of
yours." It had been raining so I had carried my notebook in an old khaki knapsack which I had left on the
spectators' bench in the back of the chamber. "And
just wanted to be sure. We've had a lot of threats,
you know, what with this income tax bill and all. You
ought to get yourself a briefcase."
 "Yeah, that would be easier for me," I said.
 "No, that would be easier on me." He smiled and
walked back to his post at the chamber doors.
 Senator Michaelson, one of the legislators who
had always shown interest and given advisory help
to NDC, spotted my NDC lapel button and introduced
himself. "I think it's great you're getting so many
people up here and involved in the political mechanisms," he said. "What you ought to do now is go out
to each of these senators' home districts and get their
constituents to talk with them. They listen to that."
 Michaelson was a good looking, middle-aged, very
genuine man. Andy had once mentioned to me that
sometime back Michaelson had come up to Nelson in
the State House lobby and asked him how things were
going. John, exhausted from driving a cab all night,
just could not muster enthusiasm. Michaelson patted

him on the back saying soothingly, "I've been hearing good things about NDC recently." And he reached into his pocket to give John ten dollars; "grocery money," as he called it, "your pants are too baggy."

The Senate chamber was beginning to fill. I studied the seating chart and identified one seated man as Senator Grimes. Grimes was a squat little man with gray hair cut short on the side. I introduced myself as a lobbyist for NDC's Open Primary Bill. "Oh, sure, we know all about NDC." Grimes was one of the Providence party machine gears. Following Nelson's instruction sheet I asked if he had any questions on the bill, any points he wanted clarified. He looked a little dumbfounded. "Just a minute." He turned around and butted into the conversation next to him. "Heh, Rodgers, what do we think of this Open Bill, NDC's thing?"

Senator Rodgers was another City Machine man. He broke away from the conversation to join Grimes and me. I introduced myself. We shook hands. "Well what's so good about it anyway?" Rodgers was short and stocky with just-cut brown hair that stuck up in back. I recited the three major points of the bill as described on the sheet - it's binding, it's proportional and no favored listings. "Well, I don't see what's so good about that. If the delegates can't get unbound from a certain candidate after the first vote at the Convention, then maybe some weak and undesirable candidate is gonna take it. You got to be able to bargain on these things. And on this proportionality thing, you know we only got twenty or thirty votes to begin with. If you go dividing up every which way, five to McCarthy, two to McGovern, ten to Muskie, or whatever, ain't nobody gonna be listening to Little Rhody." Grimes was nodding his head in the background. Rodgers ended with, "But we'll see."

I jotted down his comments, thanked him. Turning

65

around I nearly bowled over the Senate majority leader, Frank Sgambato. Senator Sgambato was a very short man with a Durante nose and thinning gray hair. He was puffing assiduously on a fat cigar. After begging his pardon I introduced myself and asked if he had questions on S-272.

"No, not really. I'm fairly familiar with the proposed legislation and have no particular questions at this time. Actually I like the theory of an open primary. It's probably good politics." Sgambato was speaking as if at a news conference so I raised my notebook and penciled down some notes on his comments. "In fact," he pointed at my notebook with his cigar, "you can quote me as supporting the bill." Pausing momentarily, "Where are you from, son?"

"I'm a student at Brown, but my hometown is near Chicago."

"Oh, Chicago. Well I was at the Chicago Convention. What a tragedy that was. But the delegates were doing a fine job. The press," he scowled at me, forgetting I was a lobbyist, not a reporter, "should have emphasized what was happening inside the hall, not out in the streets."

I interjected that it was to avoid the mistakes of the Chicago Convention that the Open Primary Bill was drafted. Sgambato was only half-listening and pretending not to listen at all. "Oh, it was a fairly open Convention. Your Mayor Daley has a lot of dissenters, but he is a fine administrator. It was just a minority of the young people that caused the problem. I want the youth to know that the Democratic Party is the one that supports their ideas. I have two grandchildren of my own, both eighteen years old. Of course, they're more politically aware than most because of my position. Most eighteen year olds don't care about politics."

The Senate chamber buzzer sounded. I thanked Senator Sgambato and joined my sack on the back bench.

COLLATING

I did more collating in the girls dorm than any
other Brown student; and when I wasn't collating, Syd
had me licking stamps, addressing envelopes, signing
letters or any number of meaningful organizational
tasks which are best delegated to monkeys, morons
or machines. This night we were preparing a packet
of S-272 literature for distribution to the Judiciary
Committee members, news media and others.

I had come over to Syd's room a little earlier than
the others to talk about some problems I was having
in researching our group independent study project.
When I entered the room Syd was sitting on the edge
of her bed talking on the phone with the receiver nes-
tled between her shoulder and cocked ear, a bright
can of Coca-cola in one hand and pencil in the other.
Without interrupting the conversation, she acknowledged
my entry with a momentary smile. I moved a stack
of notebooks from her desk chair and sat down.

Syd's room was a complete mess; clothes haphaz-
ardly thrown about, books and papers strewn across
the desk and shelves, at least five Coke cans on the
window sill and a grease stained pizza box leaning
against the waste basket. Syd, still on the phone,
stopped doodling with the pencil and began picking a
scab on her knee. She was a very unconventional girl,
so small that she didn't look anywhere near her twenty
years. Yet, she had told me that her political career
had begun at the age of fourteen when she stepped into
a local Democratic headquarters to work for the election of Lyndon Johnson. She had a certificate of appreciation for over one hundred hours of volunteer work
in that campaign to prove it. Part of her political

activism is inherited; her father was a Norman Thomas Socialist and worked in the National Youth Administration during the 1930's. I noticed a framed photograph of her parents on her desk.

During one of our many work sessions we'd had a long conversation about our political histories. Syd recalled how she had watched both 1960 political Conventions on television "so I could decide for myself. And that's not easy when you have to be in bed by 9:30." Her choice was John Kennedy and the Democrats. "His death left a deep impression in my memory." Then in 1968 she was a strong fan of Bobby Kennedy, "Though I din't work for him. He died on the night of my graduation from high school. After that I just couldn't get involved in politics. I just didn't care.

"But in college I started feeling guilty about all that like I should be doing something. So I got involved, first in the Grape Boycott then the Vietnam Moratorium Committee and then in the Student Strike. That was during my sophomore year. John Nelson asked me to stay on during the summer of '70 and work for some NDC candidates. So I did along with Andy. We got paid $46 a week. Actually I'm really glad I did it. We worked for Arcaro's election and some others running for the state Democratic committee and really got a lot accomplished."

Some others arrived to help with the collating. Syd finally got off the phone. Six of us worked at gathering, stapling and collating from nine until past midnight and we were not half finished. Nelson arrived about eleven with more letters to be stuffed, labels to be addressed and stamps to be licked. About one o'clock we discovered that we were one hundred sheets short on page eighteen. Syd said she would go to Manning Street and mimeo the missing sheets. Welcoming a chance to stop collating, I volunteered to go with her.

68

Thirty-eight East Manning Street was a bright red, subdivided house in an old residential area near the Brown campus. The students who rented it from semester to semester didn't seem to mind the broken window panes or whining furnace blower. Plus they were willing to pay higher rents than working tenants, so the landlord took a laissez-faire attitude toward their activities, within the bounds of reason, of course. From what Syd told me, the NDC had on several occasions come close to transgressing even those borders.

I parked my car under a street lamp on Manning. Syd and I used a flashlight to make our way to the back of the unlighted house. I pulled open the unhinged basement door and we went down, Syd warning me about a missing step. The basement had the unpleasant odor of a cat's litter box in addition to being cold and damp. Syd pulled the light string. The place looked like a Twelfth Century dungeon - crumbling gray cement walls and the rusting iron of a fuel oil tank and furnace. Tucked beneath the wooden stairs was an aged Gestetner mimeograph surrounded by piles of waste paper. Syd went right to work. She inked the machine, rummaged through a cardboard box to find the right stencil, stacked the paper and had page eighteen flying out of the machine within minutes.

I asked her how long NDC had been renting this place. She said last summer John had sublet the upstairs, without the landlord's knowledge, from some student tenants to use as a campaign office. "The fun began," Syd smiled, "when John tried to get some phones installed." A private residence phone is billed at a lower rate than an office phone. John, working on a shoe string budget, had the phone installed on a private residence billing. The telephone company quickly caught on and squealed to the landlord. The landlord raised the students' rent, which wasn't too bad, but John still needed a phone.

One of the neighbors, "a professor who shall remain nameless," agreed to have a phone installed in his house and then let John run a line over to his office. With a spool of telephone cable in hand, John hung out of windows, climbed trees and ducked under fences. Unfortunately, one of the less sympathetic neighbors objected to having telephone cable laid across his vegetable garden. He threatened to call the telephone company, but instead, cut the wire. John spliced the wire that night, but again the neighbor cut it. John would return every night splicing and burying the wire or trying to conceal it with tar. But each day the neighbor would find it and cut it again. So the phone was always dead during the day but working at night.

Another time, Syd told me, they spotted a phone company repair truck at the home of the professor to whom the phone was charged. The professor's wife stalled the repairman asking him to return in an hour. She notified John who bundled the phone in a rag and returned it to the professor's house for the day.

Syd and I quickly finished mimeographing and returned to the collating "party." It was nearly 3 a.m. before I got to bed.

FINANCE MEETING

March 11

John informed me of an executive committee meeting. He suggested I might find it interesting to attend. The meeting was held at the home of John Sapinsly located in the wealthier part of Providence near Benevolent Street. It was a large, expensive house with a doorbell that chimed like Big Ben. Sapinsly was in his fifties. A former executive of a Rhode Island firm he left business to get his PhD from Brown University and become an economics professor.

"Welcome, come on in," he greeted me at the door. "You're the first to arrive. Go on downstairs, have some coffee." Sapinsly dressed modishly young for his age. In the Northeastern liberal tradition he had a compulsion for the current cause. And like a good businessman he saw politics, perhaps accurately so, in terms of contacts and contributions.

Martin Malinou was next to arrive. Martin was a local bachelor lawyer with a modest one-man office on South Street. For the past two years he had been the NDC treasurer and for about that long had been looking for a replacement. A little overweight and balding, he was slipping into middle age unnoticed. That almost changed however when he decided in 1970 to run for US Senator taking on the invincible John O. Pastore. Martin never even made it onto the primary ballot but he did create some interesting litigation which he doggedly carried all the way to the US Supreme Court. Being refused by the Supreme Court was a great point of pride for Martin.

Next to arrive was Abbot Gleason. Tom, nobody called him Abbot, had just begun his teaching career as an associate professor in the history department at Brown. He taught Russian history. Extremely articulate and witty, Tom had received about as good an education as is possible in this society. Undergraduate at Harvard, studied at Heidelberg and Berlin as a Fulbright scholar and returned to Harvard to complete his graduate studies. He came from a well-to-do, government service oriented family. Yet he, his attractive wife and their baby son lived in middle-class austerity in a small row house on John Street near campus. Tom looked like a Tolstoy character or the young revolutionary in Pasternack's ZHAVAGO. He was tall and lean with strong dark eyes and longish brown hair combed back and across to conceal balding.

Nervous (who wouldn't be with all that education) he constantly smoked cheap little cigars like Erics and worse yet, inhaled them.

John, Syd and Andy were the last to arrive. John opened the meeting by announcing that Hogan had finally appointed a task force to study election law reform. John was hardly satisfied; "Two years after Harris' letter he decides to appoint a commission. This guy is incredible. He sits on the whole thing for two years and now, with our bill in committee and the session about to adjourn, he appoints a task force to study the problem. And he tells the Judiciary Committee that he hopes they'll hold off passing on the bill until this commission has a chance to make recommendations. You know how long that will be."

John read the list of commission members: Mayor Joseph A. Doorley, Jr., National Committeeman; Mrs. Isabelle Leeds, National Committeewoman; Joseph Bevilacqua, House Speaker; William Fecteau, Jr., deputy Senate majority leader; Anthony Arico, Jr., Barrington party chairman; Joseph Scanlon, an aide to Rep. St. Germain; Stanton Abrams, campaign worker for Governor Licht; Dr. Jay Goodman, political science professor; Francis Boyle, a Newport attorney; Normand Theriault, a party activist from Woonsocket; Edward Hughes, Jr., a state committee member; and Joseph Keough, Jr., a political associate of Mayor Burns of Pawtucket. John had also been appointed to the commission. But in doing so Hogan had made sure that he would be relatively isolated amidst a group of party regulars.

John moved on to organizational matters. He asked for comments on the idea of purchasing an addressograph machine to automatically address envelopes. This sounded like a fantastic idea to me. John's regular method of addressing other than handwriting was to

cut a stencil of an often used address then run a dozen
or so envelopes through the mimeo filing them for future mailings. Sapinsly, sitting on a bar stool in front
of John, spoke abruptly, "How much?" Nelson, double
checking his notes, said they were selling for two to
three hundred dollars. "Hell, we can do better than
that on a common office machine like an addressograph. Go to one of those waste brokers. They've
always got some used addressographs around. What
else?"

John steamed ahead. "Well, we could also use an
offset printing press. Nothing big, just one of those
table top models."

"And what do they cost?" Sapinsly interrogated.

"Around a thousand dollars."

"And what are our current printing expenses?"

"I'd say at least eighty dollars a month and that
is likely to rise in the next few months."

Martin, who had been puffing attentively on his
briar wood pipe, suddenly leaned forward in his chair.
"I don't know John. It sounds as though we are perhaps advancing a little too quickly here. Spreading
ourselves into too many areas of specialization. Personally, I think, all in all, it is cheaper to send the
material out."

Sapinsly nodded his head. "He's probably right.
For the time being at least. Let's forget it."

Nelson, undaunted, moved on the other financial
matters - his salary. John, who had often put in twelve
hour days and usually was doing NDC business seven
days a week, had, over the last two years, received
a total salary of eight hundred dollars. "How he's
done it," Gleason piped up, "is the mystery of Orms
Street. And he doesn't even collect food stamps!"
John appreciated that. Encouraged he went on. He
felt a salary of $5,200 a year for the executive director
was minimal.

"And you ought to make that retroactive for the
past two years," Gleason offered.

"Yes, that's what I'd been thinking," Nelson res-
poned quickly. "So that means $5,200 per year for a
four year period or $10,400 per year for the next two
years. Plus I'd expect an equivalent salary of $5,200
per year for three summer staff workers. That would
mean $1300 per staff member for a three month period."

Martin, who as treasurer had watched the NDC bank
account for the past two years, winced but said nothing.
Sapinsly still looked flabergasted by John's comment
that he was receiving a salary of four hundred dollars
per year for the past two years. Tom put out another
Tiperillo and made a motion that John receive the
salary he had requested and that funds be appropriated
during the summer to pay for a three member staff.
Who could possibly object?

The meeting moved on to the consideration of NDC's
future role in Rhode Island politics. "The question as
I see it," John said, "is should NDC become a local
office for a Presidential candidate like McGovern?"

"Absolutely not!" Gleason spoke vociferously.
"That's putting the cart before the donkey. It's just
too soon to commit the organization to one candidate.
Not only would we splinter the existing membership,
but we'd probably eliminate whatever effectiveness
we have in matters of electoral reform." Beautifully
spoken. I agreed completely.

"But it'd be a hell of a lot easier to collect dues
if we had someones picture posted on the front door,"
Sapinsly spoke pragmatically.

We discussed the idea for a few minutes then let
it drop without coming to any real consensus. It was
getting late so we closed the meeting and all went our
separate ways.

S-272 HEARING

March 16
    The Senate Judiciary Committee hearing on S-272
was scheduled for three p.m. At one-thirty Nelson
called me to ask if I would please mimeo some material for the hearing - last minute amendments he wanted
to present to the committee. I picked up the stencils
at Orms Street then drove to Manning.
    I mimeoed until two-thirty then quickly put on my
tweed suit which I had stuffed into a knapsack and
stored in the back seat of my car. I walked up the
marble steps of the State House front entrance about
two-fifty carrying a loosely stacked bundle of papers,
my black cased Miranda 35mm and a cassette tape
recorder.
    The hearing room was filling quickly. John was
scurrying about setting up his microphone in front of
the witness stand and another on the committee bench.
Senator Michaelson, chairman of the Judiciary Committee, had already taken his seat but had not yet
gavelled the hearing to order. Nelson grabbed the
mimeo sheets from me and asked me to plug the mike
leads into the recorder. In doing so I discovered that
I had forgotten to bring the cassette tapes. Dropping
all pretense to decorum at this point, I ran from the
State House to my car, drove quickly back to the dorm,
found the tapes and within fifteen minutes was back in
the hearing room, breathing hard but with tapes in
hand.
    The hearing had just begun. It seemed I hadn't
missed anything of importance. The recorder was
running smoothly, but to be sure it was picking up
properly, I stopped it and pushed the play-back button,
" . . . and by the Four Tops some real grooving sound,

yeah, on a sunny afternoon. This is W-I-C-E, your
Providence rock sta. . ." Calamity! The tape recorder was picking up a radio station and not Senator
Michaelson's first reading of S-272. How or why I
could not figure out, but it was impossible to tape the
hearings. I shrugged my shoulders, made some in-
comprehensibly coded signals to Nelson and circulated
around the small crowd snapping photographs.

NDC had gathered an impressive collection of wit-
nesses. Marjorie Stenberg, a member of the executive
committee of the Republican state committee spoke in
favor of the bill. An ex-NDC member, the young state
representative Jim Aukerman spoke for the bill as did
William Barbour, a long time liberal from Bristol.
Isabel Leeds, the Democratic National Committeewoman,
said she also endorsed the Open Primary with possible
reservations on eliminating the   twenty-six month rule.

The first witness to voice oppostion to the bill was
Maurice Hendel, assistant to the Secretary of State in
charge of law revision and author of the 1969 Licht
primary bill. Hendel had the look of a party regular,
paunchy and graying,   reluctant to answer anything too
quickly. "This bill is idealistic, to say the least, but
unworkable, " was his pronouncement. "Look here for
example, on page three." The senators fanned through
their papers. "It's just plain impossible to implement
this section. It doesn't allow enough time to examine
nomination papers prior to the primary."

Nelson came to his feet and asked if he might address
himself to that; "If you'll look at the amendment sheet
I passed out at the beginning of the hearing you'll see
that we already corrected   that problem by moving
the filing date up two weeks. Do you have a copy of
this sheet Mr. Hendel?"

Hendel blustered a bit, then said, "Oh , yes, I see
it now. Well, yes, that may be alright although this is

something new. I'll have to look it over first. But
what about this other section over on page four, the
part about the distribution of ballots. Now that's just
plain impossible. I've been working with voting machines for a long time and I got a real feel for the
logistics. This is impossible." His second pronouncement.

Hendel directed his comment to Nelson so John rose
again reading the section under question. "Could be,"
he said, "but that section is part of the old bill which
we left unchanged in ours. You drafted that section
yourself, Mr. Hendel." Hendel read it again and
looked flabergasted. He looked back at John with a
sullen smirk on his lips, raised his hand from the
witness box railing as though he was about to say something, then remained silent.

Martin Malinou took the witness stand. He spoke
against the preferred ballot postion for party endorsed
candidates which S-272 would eliminate. Martin was
a very articulate and dramatic witness standing tall
in a silken, well-tailored dark blue suit accenting his
receding jet black hair. He gripped the oak railing
with both hands while the late afternoon sun burst
through the lead pane windows behind him. From
the committee bench a senator interrupted Martin to
say that he could not believe ballot position made any
difference, "I, for example, have been third and even
fourth on the ballot and still got elected." Martin rode
right over that comment treating it as so much political
bravado, going on to a detailed explanation of his Supreme Court case. Another senator interrupted to
point out that Martin had lost his argument in the
Rhode Island courts.

Martin retaliated with lawyeresque coolness; "That
decision was made on a hot August day by a judge who
was once state committee chairman."

Senator Michaelson, chairman of the hearing and a Democrat in good standing, was not about to let Martin's statement go unchallenged. He stopped Martin in his tracks and chastised him for implying that Judge Giannini's former position as Democratic state committee chairman may have prejudiced him in a court case. "In point of fact," Michaelson said emphatically, "Judge Giannini undoubtedly used his previous experience to bring him to a fairer judgement."

Co-sponsor of the bill, Harold Arcaro, took the stand momentarily speaking in vague generalities about the need for reform. When pressed on some fine-print points of the legislation, he stated that he hadn't actually drafted the bill, that the authorship was strictly NDC's. He referred the complicated questions to Nelson who answered from the floor. Questions on proportionality, binding of the delegates' votes and voter qualifications were complex and difficult to answer. The hearing ended with more confusion about S-272 than answers.

BUGGED

April 13

Nelson was a character of many faces. Just when I thought he was taking all these political shenanigans too seriously, he surprised me with an out-and-out outrageous sense of humor. He had called me asking that I return his tape recorder which he needed to tape his draft board hearing set for the next day. When I arrived at his apartment that evening, John and a friend were at the kitchen table having a dinner of steamed Uncle Ben's rice along with a gallon of Gallo burgandy. The friend was Fred Spar, one of John's ex-roommates.

Fred looked like a younger Fred McMurray with heavy
jaw and deep voice. Since graduating, Fred had been
teaching in a public grammar school in New York's
Chinatown. He had returned to Providence during
his Easter holiday to help NDC.

John's junior high school hi-fi, with one dog-eared
speaker, was on the kitchen floor blaring out some un-
familiar, brassy music. It was marching music,
hardly anything one would normally have with dinner
and so loud that it was impossible to converse. Motioning
that he'd turn it down, John got up doing so with the
aid of crutches which were lying on the floor beside
him. He hobbled on one foot over to the record player,
took the record off the turn table and held up its jacket;
"The Red Army Ensemble - Military Music of the
People's Republic of China."

"Incredible," I thought. "Simply incredible."

"We've been hearing some suspicious clicking
noises on the phones recently. If they've got the placed
bugged, this should give 'em an earfull."

Trying to assimilate two shocks at once I asked,
"What the hell happened to your foot?"

John said he had sprained it in a skiing accident
that wekeend. The doctor had wrapped it in an elastic
bandage and advised that he would be on crutches for
a month, maybe longer. What a strange turn of events.
John's draft board, which had, after the usual reticence,
granted him a conscientious objector status, had as
yet failed to decide on alternative service. John had
been suggesting all along that NDC work be accepted
in lieu of military service. The board found that hard
to swallow. But their final decision on what to do with
the strange case of John Nelson was coming up at six-
fifteen the following evening. They'd have to make up
their minds then because within a month John would
be twenty-seven years old and effectively out of their

reach. Now, with John's foot injury, any action against him would have to be delayed past his birthday, which meant safety.

After leaving John and Fred, I drove back to the campus, stopping at Syd' to return a borrowed book. She had already received the "good news" of John's sprained ankle. We talked for awhile then I said something which elicited a strange reaction from Syd. Casually I asked, "Whatever happened to that other NDC summer staff worker? I haven't seen him around this semester. John was his name, wasn't it?"

Syd, behaving oddly, said, "John? Oh, he graduated. Had some trouble with the local draft board. They refused his CO request and about two weeks ago he finally got his draft notice." Syd abruptly turned on the radio to some whining country western station. Speaking softly she said that John had left for Canada as soon as he had received his notice. She had just received a letter from him saying he'd found a job in Toronto. He had enclosed five Canadian dollars in the letter as a contribution to NDC - "So maybe I can come home someday soon." Looking around as if someone were spying on us, Syd said she had been hearing some suspicious noises on her phone recently and she was nervous, suspecting that maybe her room was bugged. "Who knows?!" she concluded.

I left Syd's room depressed, feeling uncomfortably uncertain. I wondered if maybe Syd and Nelson weren't just playing some paranoiac childish games with all this talk of wiretapping and room bugging. Or, maybe, if they weren't absolutely correct in assigning the most sinister motives and actions to a government which was everyday, all around, reaching into the personal dreams of young people,and casting their souls onto the rocks, chasing them into exile or dropping them into the hell of Vietnam.

I walked over to the John Hay Library and up to
the third floor Harris Collection. A quiet, isolated,
monestary-like room, it was a good place to retreat
and think out difficulties. I checked out two books
of poetry, AND TIME BEGAN and OTHER THINGS
AND THE AARDVARK, reading both as I sat at a
long wooden table. It was comforting to me to know
that a poet can metamorphise even the most trying of
times into a meaningful and positive expression.

DUMP NIXON RALLY

April 18
       Potential political candidates were testing their
strength on nationwide platforms. In Providence an
ad hoc organization called Citizens For Alternatives
Now (CAN) had planned a "Dump Nixon" rally on the
State House lawn. Invited speakers included Democrats Edmund Muskie and Birch Bayh.
       The NDC did not take a role in this rally other
than to lend its scant membership list to the CAN
telephone canvassers. Nelson did see the rally, however, as an excellent opportunity to make contact
with at least two of the Democratic Presidential hope-
fuls. A couple weeks before their scheduled arrival
in Providence, Nelson had contacted both Bayh's and
Muskie's offices requesting an interview while they
were in Providence. Muskie, an early front runner,
delayed as long as possible. Finally his staff responded
writing that they sincerely regretted the Senator's
stringent schedule left no time for an interview while
in Providence. Awfully sorry and all that.
       Bayh, the Indiana longshot, was quick to accept
the offer. His schedule was also "stringent," but he
made time squeezing the NDC interview into the back

seat of his limousine during the short drive from the Downtown Biltmore to the rally.

Lanky John, on crutches, tape recorder strapped over his shoulder, stood nervously in front of the bustling Biltmore. He was fidgetting with his tie, then pressing against the corner of his suit coat trying to squeeze out that last wrinkle. Nelson had arranged for three of NDC's more prominent members, John Sapinsly, Carol Henkle and William Barbour, to join him in interviewing Bayh. They were already seated in the back of the dark blue limousine when the Senator emerged from the hotel.

In a flurry of movement, Bayh, a tall, handsome and well-groomed man, walked across the sidewalk, enveloped in an entourage of clean-cut young men. One of his staff members introduced Nelson to the Senator while another aide opened the limousine door. John blushed from the excitement of it all while the Senator remained untouchable, dignified yet personable. Like a sultan gathering up a crippled pauper from the curb, Bayh helped Nelson into the limousine. One aide closed the door while two others got into the front seat. On cue, the uniformed state troopers stopped traffic and the long, dark limousine glided away from the curb. The synchronization was hypnotizing. It flowed integrally like a ballet.

Once inside the car John introduced the other NDC members and, with the Senator's permission, turned on his tape recorder. He had spent days preparing his questions:

Nelson - From reading the CONGRESSIONAL RECORD, it appears that the South Vietnamese election in '67 was the turning point in your thinking and at that time you said that the US foreign policy needed some changes in attitude and that formally it had been based simply

82

on slogans. Could you elaborate on what you felt those slogans or tenets of the Johnson philosophy were that needed to be replaced?

Senator Bayh – I don't think it was just a Johnson philosophy. I think it was back even prior to World War Two or at least after World War Two, where we felt that it was our business personally to dictate what happened in every little country all over the world. Sort of the world policeman philosophy, that if we thought it was right that this axiomatically made it right for those that lived in the community or in an area of the world. I don't think that it can be limited to Lyndon Johnson. I think that was just sort of the feeling of the United States.

It was not just the election in Vietnam. I started having real concern then but what really convinced me was when I was over there in January '68. When I saw the degree to which our country had permitted itself to become involved in every aspect of life politically, economically, militarily. And you talk to a lot of the guys there who saw the degree to which we really weren't effecting the kind of policy most of us were led to believe we were effecting. In other words, the business of self-determination and better life and the hearts and minds of people. That really convinced me that there had to be some change. I mean Vietnam is a can of worms. You come back from there not absolutely certain who you can believe because there are so many different stories told there.

Nelson – Senator Muskie made a speech last February in which he stated that he'd like to see negotiated anything that is negotiable, but he didn't define what he felt was negotiable. What do you feel is negotiable if we in fact remove all the troops?

83

Senator Bayh - Well, you know, I think negotiations are doomed to failure if you start out with a list of things that are non-negotiable. I think you can say anything is negotiable and then you see. Saying it's negotiable doesn't mean that you're going to agree with the other fellow on all issues, but I think you at least need to enter negotiations with good faith saying we are willing to discuss everything and in the final analysis realizing that some of the things are not our province to negotiate. I take a dim view of us sitting down here or in Paris trying to determine just what kind of government is going to rule South Vietnam for the next ten years. I wonder if maybe the South Vietnamese people shouldn't have something to say about that.

Nelson - If all the troops are removed from Vietnam, do you see a role for us any longer at the negotiating table?

Senator Bayh - Well, if we can, as one of the major world powers, help the parties to stop fighting. One of the major concerns I've had with the present policy is that it's based on the premise that fighting is all right, war is all right, as long as yellow people are being killed instead of white people. And I don't buy that philosophy. As an American and as a US Senator, I am more concerned when American young men are being killed than when others, but I still have deep concern when we don't make a maximum effort to find peace, not just find a way for others to fight. (The limousine arrives at the State House.) Thank you, John. Anytime you want to pursue this I'll be glad to.

I walked from the Biltmore to the State House mingling with the crowd for awhile before finally taking a

a place on the far west slope of the front lawn. It was
a blustery, gray day. The trees were still just winter
skeletons and the wide lawn stretched brown and flat
like army canvass. The crowd, some said six thousand,
others eighteen thousand, huddled in the center of the
lawn in front of the capitol's white marble steps. The
speakers stood at the landing. Massed people cascaded
down the stone flowing onto the lawn like hot pulled taffy.
At the perimeter of the crowd, away from the rostrum's
magnetism, people came and went, children played
tag and dogs barked. One wild-eyed radical ran around
with a red flag on the end of a broomstick while another
marched up and down waving the Stars and Stripes. A
police helicopter battered the air overhead. Still higher,
a piper cub dragged a banner reading "YAF Asks Why
Help Hanoi?"

Everyone was dressed warmly against the chill
and dampness. Some had wrapped themselves in blan-
kets. Blue, the color of youth, dominated the green -
the blue of jeans and levi jackets, blue windbreakers,
trench coats and stocking caps.

Allard Lowenstein, the long time anti-War strategist and instigator of this rally, welcomed the people
to "Providence, the Riviera of New England." The
renegade California Republican, Paul McCloskey spoke
about the block buster bombs used in Vietnam "which
can destroy twenty-five acres leaving a piece of shrap-
nel in every square yard." Birch Bayh developed the
theme of the War's destructive power at home. "The
Vietnam War," he said, "has caused a lot of people
to lose faith in the United States." Muskie, the party
regulars' favorite, was greeted by sporadic boos and
some chanting. He offered a droll speech with the
diction and grammar of James Fennimore Cooper;
"The real nightmare of recrimination will come if more
Americans and Vietnamese die for a no longer com-

pelling reason." John Haynes of the AFL-CIO was there to speak for the hard-hats; George Wiley of the National Welfare Rights Organization to speak for the poor and oppressed; and beautiful Black Congresswoman Bella Abzug topped off the rally with a smashing new hat.

After leaving Bayh's limousine, Nelson had made his way past the guards to the speakers' rostrum. Peter Yarough of Peter, Paul and Mary, was at the podium warming the audience with Seegar-style protest songs. John spotted Muskie. Microphone in hand, he stepped forward and started talking:

Nelson - Have you got time for one question? My name is John Nelson from the New Democratic Coalition here.

Senator Muskie - I understand.

Nelson - I read your speech of February 23. I believe it was in Pennsylvania. And you said you'd like to negotiate whatever is negotiable. Do you see a role for us at the negotiating table after the troops are out? After they've all been removed, is there still a use for us at the negotiating table? And exactly what would be negotiable?

Senator Muskie - Hi Birch. (Senator Birch Bayh walks past.) No, no. My point in that speech was that if we set a deadline for withdrawal and negotiate before then...

Nelson - I see.

Senator Muskie - . . . these points: the prisoners of war, the safe withdrawal of our troops and perhaps even a political arrangement. In other words, in my judgement the setting of a deadline would enhance the possibility of negotiating those things that are important to us,

Nelson - Before that time?

Senator Muskie - before that time.

Nelson - Yeah, but you still adhere to the end of this year to get all the troops out?

Senator Muskie - That's right.

Nelson - Or if the present occupant of the White House, (at this point Peter Yarough's singing was increasing in volume making it difficult for the conversants to hear one another.)

Senator Muskie - It's a little difficult to conduct a conversation at this point. Why don't we wait? (The lyrics of Peter's song, THE GREAT MANDELLA, grow stronger and stronger; "Take you place on the Great Mandella as it moves through your brief moment of time. Win or lose now, you must choose now. . .")

Nelson - Thank you very much Senator.

NDC REGIONAL MEETINGS

With the spring thaw came an awakened political
awareness in the Northeastern states. The local NDC
groups which had lay dorment or limited themselves
to state affairs, were turning now to the approaching
national primaries less than a year away. Marvin
Madeson had called an NDC national conference in
St. Louis on April 3, 1971, but had to cancel those
plans for lack of registrants. The Northeastern NDCs,
the most active and concentrated, decided to go ahead
with their own regional conference.

April 17
    The meeting was held at the New York state NDC
headquarters in the less-than-elegant Henry Hudson
Hotel on West Fifty-Seventh Street. About twenty-five
NDC members were present representing Deleware,
Maryland, New Jersey, New York, Pennsylvania, and
Virginia. Tom Gleason, myself and a perky, bright-
eyed, though non-political, friend, Sharon Davis, represented Rhode Island.
    Though the New York NDC had a large membership
and had wielded considerable influence in the '70 state
and Congressional elections, their downtown headquarters
suggested anything but success. They rented a four-
room suite in the hotel with cracking plaster walls,
hissing steam pipe radiators, dark-stained, threadbare
carpets and church-basement folding furniture. But
it served the purpose.
    Dan Collins, a middle-aged, soft spoken law pro-
fessor, was chairman of the host state's NDC and pre-
sided over the meeting. No one had known exactly
what to expect when the invitations went out so the
meeting began without a formal agenda or any definite

direction. The state representatives introduced themselves to one another and gave a rundown of their local organizations and activities. Marv Madeson, as national chairman, was asked to give an impromptu state of the Coalition address.

Marv was very much a Midwesterner. In his fifties, he was a conservative dresser with mirror-shined shoes, a dark blue suit and carefully barbered hair. Though he had a lawyeresque staccato speech and acerbity of wit, it was tempered by a Missouri reserve. He didn't volunteer comments. He would listen stonefaced, arms crossed, to even the most inane comments. His view of the organization hadn't changed since the '70 national convention in Chicago. Money was still the major crisis facing NDC. "Throughout the country I find a general lack of funds," he understated. Looking at the progress of state organizations individually, he commented, "In Iowa, we are the Democratic Party; Wisconsin . . . healthy; Ohio. . . they can do more; Illinois. . . they have a tough fight around Chicago; New Mexico. . . surprisingly active." He presented a very restrained, though realistic picture of the national organization - there was something out there, but it wasn't moving too much.

Some of the others offered the usual fund raising gripes. "How the hell can we finance a 'delegate selection' campaign or a 'primary reform' campaign? People want to give their money to some guy's grinning, lying face," one cynic said.

Tom Gleason was more helpful; "Perhaps I am more pessimistic than most - fund raising is no bed of roses in Rhode Island. But we are not going to be able to get more money unless, as a national organization, we look better."

The rest of the group picked up on that theme and discussed the preparation of a coherent, national policy -

a set of issues upon which to judge candidates. We voted to hold a regional issues convention the following month in New York to compose an NDC position paper as the first step in solidifying the national ranks.

May 15
 The second NDC meeting was a raucous affair with the heart-pounding controversy and fast moving action that no lifelong Republican can even imagine. Fifty people crowded into the Henry Hudson suite this time, some in Brooks Brothers' tweeds, others in patched levis and scuffed boots with frizzy hair that exploded from their scalps and engulfed their ears. Mostly, though, those in attendance were the devoted middle-class liberals, the nouveau politicos, college educated and clerical, approaching politics as some approach sailing, with zeal and a yearning for excitement heightened by a quasi-religious seriousness.
 Dan Collins, puffing professorially on a meerschaum pipe, gavelled the meeting to order from behind a plywood table. But it wasn't until New York's young secretary, a dark-eyed, sexy brunette, stood up to read the minutes of the April meeting that the representatives took notice and stopped slurping from their Dixie coffee cups.
 The major item coming from the April meeting, other than a call to the May meeting, was a letter to Lawrence O'Brien, Chairman of the Democratic National Committee, requesting that he convene a Democratic National Convention in 1971 which would "serve as the foundation for a 1972 Presidential campaign." Such a platform convention was necessary, the letter continued, because "it is our firm belief that to win in 1972, the Democratic Party must speak out clearly on the issues of concern to the people of this nation. Moreover, the issues as developed, must

begin at and be responsive to the grass roots." Nothing of this sort had ever been convened before and, of course, not one of those twenty-five NDC'ers signing the letter, except the hopelessly naive, expected it to be convened this time either. But it was a very clever way of exerting pressure on O'Brien who, as Marv Madeson had said earlier, had been "ducking" him for months.

One of the attendees who rose to laud this approach was Jerome Grossman, head of the very influential Massachusett's anti-War organization, Mass Pax. Grossman was a lion among the usually sheepish peace-liberals. In stature he was imposing, over six feet tall, broad shouldered, an iron jaw, tanned, flawless bald head and a relentless, unchallengeable stare. But it was his booming voice and colorful diction that made him a natural orator. "If and when the Democratic Party has a platform," Grossman spoke from in front of his chair in the middle of the room, "upon which we, as peace-oriented liberals can comfortably stand, then and only then can we endorse a candidate. Our only hope in the accomplishment of NDC goals is in marrying endorsement to platform. I would like to see our clout as the heart of the anti-War movement. Unless we organize and set the stage now, the strongest peace candidates will chew each other up in '72 just like Kennedy and McCarthy in '68."

Phil Sipser, another unabashed orator, took the floor next injecting some unexpected, probably mis-placed, discussion. Sipser, a gray-haired New York liberal who had been with NDC at its inception, spoke loudly in a lecturing, demanding tone reminiscent of a party lieutenant's instructions to a rank-and-file gathering. "Before we start working out plans for endorsing candidates in an election more than a year away," Sipser wagged his finger at the group, "let's

not forget the issues right now. The Black Caucus
last week issued a statement which I have here and
would like to read." He did; all of it. In it Carl
Stokes and other Black Democrats accused the Democratic Party of not allowing them their rightful place
in the Party. Perhaps the NDC should have received
the same accusation; as I double checked the room I
didn't see a single Black face. Factually, however,
the absence of Blacks in the NDC leadership was not
the result of any invidious discrimination on cur part.
It was solely the choice of the Blacks themselves.
Sipser's request for this NDC conference to endorse
the Black Caucus statement may well have emanated
from sincere, altruistic motives, but it was side-
tracking the stated NDC agenda, keeping us from discussing the platform strategy.

Fortunately, Grossman rose to put the issue in
perspective and snuff out the interference. "This,"
he boomed out impatietnly, "is typical left-wing
meeting rhetoric. We're here to discuss agenda and
work on organization. A letter to O'Brien in support
of Blacks is nothing more than self-serving rhetoric.
We haven't the time to engage in such prattle. I move
we close this discussion and move on with the business
at hand, Mr. Chairman." That was the consensus
and Phil Sipser indignantly sat down.

Ken Bode, research director of the McGovern
Commission on Delegate Selection, had been invited
to the meeting to offer his assessment of Party reform
to date and its potential. Nearing thirty, Bode had
the mannerisms of an aspiring Washington lawyer.
His speech was rapid yet articulate, he used his hands
freely, outlining ideas or emphasizing a point. In dress,
he was extremely casual wearing a bulky-knit, white
sweater and gray slacks. He had the appearance of
an experienced, though aging, student activist , his

still-bushy, brown hair combed down concealing a gradually receding hairline.

After the McGovern Commission finished its business and dissolved, Bode continued the fight organizing the Center For Political Reform in Washinton, D.C., which acted as a watch-dog, reformists lobby group. He'd been participating in the law suits calling for reapportionment of the Democratic National Committee plus he had been traveling across the country coordinating the state reform efforts.

"Some of the states are slow to act, too slow," he said, resting against a chair. "The only message I can offer is that if you let it slide now, you must be prepared to live with it later. There's a lot of regulars who are resisting. Lou Davis, Connally's right-hand man in Texas and a member of the McGovern Commission, worked hard against reform and he's just one of a thousand examples." Get organized was Bode's message - create and fund a legal task force to prepare briefs for challenges and help other unequiped states. Bode had a plane to catch in an hour, another meeting in Michigan, so he concluded by answering a few questions then ducking into an adjacent room. I followed him wanting to get the address of his organization in Washington.

Bode was a man in a hurry. Like a perfomer between acts, he sat in the back room wiping the perspiration and oil from his forehead with a wet Kleenex. He looked up at me momentarily, "Yeah, what is it?" He lifted his bulky white sweater and dabbed under his arm pits with the Kleenex. He recited the address while I scribbled it down. I asked if he felt an NDC endorsement would be of much help to any candidate. "Fat chance," he grunted. "First of all, there is no way the national structure, at least what I have seen of it, is gonna get organized enough to endorse, and secondly, unless they get a lot more members, who cares who they endorse? Listen, the only way NDC is gonna help is helping themselves on the state level. When Rhode Island has prepared itself to challenge, contact me and we'll offer whatever advise we can. It's really up to the local groups, though."

I returned to the meeting which, with considerable ballyhoo and confusion, was organizing a couple more committees.

WAR IS STILL THE ISSUE

May 12

"John, you just don't seem to understand. The War is not an issue any longer. Nixon's defused it. Kaput. That's it. Forget it. We'll never be able to rally support around that issue." John sat calmly on the puce sofa in Jack Indeck's living room, listening to this lecture from one of the executive committee members. "If we are going to build NDC in this state let's do it around an issue that's touching the people - economics." John looked around the room, his sharp blue eyes resting momentarily on each of the dozen persons at the meeting. "Why, hell, this inflation has got the housewives up in arms. Or let's find a real candidate, somebody with looks and some old-fashioned charisma. I don't like to admit it, but if we're gonna knock 'em off their feet in '72, we gotta have a face. That's what they want."

John held back a few moments hoping someone else would respond. But the other executive committee members were sullenly silent. It was near the end of a late evening meeting, nearly nine o'clock. A couple of the members, particularly the women, were fidgety, worrying about the babysitter. A few others were

stealing glances at their watches, concerned about
the long drive home.

John had begun the meeting a couple hours before
with a status report on the Open Primary Bill. Actually,
it was more of a eulogy. The Hogan Commission, acting
as the state party's primary reform task force, had
voted to retain the winner-take-all aspect of the Rhode
Island primary, squelching NDC's plan for allotment
of delegates in proportion to the Presidential candidates'
vote. This had literally knocked the stuffing out of
S-272. The commission's goal was to totally bypass
S-272 and draft their own legislation. In fact, a skeleton
bill had already been submitted to the House Judiciary
Committee to serve as the vehicle for that legislation.

With the Open Primary Bill dead, the NDC would
have to choose another path to get their delegates to
the Convention. The strategy was still in the formative
stage - but as John saw it then, NDC could conduct its
own delegate selection convention choosing a propor-
tionately bound delegate slate which would run as "uncommitted" on the primary ballot. If the uncommitted
slate won, the delegates would then go to the national
Convention and vote in the same proportion as the votes
cast for the Presidential candidates at the NDC state
convention. And even if the uncommitted NDC slate
did not win in the state primary, they could still challenge and possibly displace the regular state delegation
on the grounds that the primary was not conducted in
accordance with the new delegate selection rules of the
Democratic Party.

Nelson suggested that NDC immediately begin edu-
cating the voters to the challenge procedure and that
it initiate a search for challenge -slate delegates. "And
even more importantly," John added with emphasis,
"if we are ever going to elect a President who really
will end this War, then one of our main functions during

this time should be to help our members see who is and who is not a peace candidate." He unveiled his Operation Peace President.

For weeks John had been working on a concise, inclusive statement of policy regarding the War. His Policy to End the War was drawn basically from George McTurnan Kahin's 1969 book THE UNITED STATES IN VIETNAM, with substantiating and updating evidence taken from statements made in WAR/PEACE REPORT and news reports. Basically, the policy called for the setting of an absolute military withdrawal date and the minimizing of US political presence in preparation for the October '71 Vietnamese elections, The aim of the policy was to extract the US from Vietnam in such a way as to restore political self-determination to the South Vietnamese people.

With a firm NDC Policy to End the War established, Nelson then prepared a list of "Questions for Presidential Prospects on Vietnam." The questions zeroed in on the absolute issues and details regarding such things as economic aid to Saigon, acceptance of Viet Cong ceasefire offers, the Paris negotiations. Nelson submitted these questions to the announced Presidential candidates Birch Bayh, Harold Hughes, George McGovern, and Edmund Muskie. His goal was to dig under the general and, in some cases, equivocal statements of those "anti-War" Democrats and establish the tenets of their individual policies, thereby comparing and contrasting the candidates on that singel issue - War. Besides soliciting written policy statements from each candidate, John also dug into the CONGRESSIONAL RECORD pulling out all the statements on Vietnam ever made by these four Presidential contenders, arranging comparative excerpts in "Presidential Candidates' Stands on Vietnam." He prefaced that NDC paper with the following chart:

	Bayh	Hughes	McGovern	Muskie
Major statements:	1	3	6	0
Resolutions, amendments sponsored:	1	1	1	0
Column inches of actual statement:	125"	136"	349"	0
Inches of material introduced:	0	342"	1936"	0

Nelson's goal was simply to "cut the crap" surrounding the Presidential candidates' stands on Vietnam. He had done a brilliant job in creatively forcing the facts to the surface, presenting these in coherent statement papers to the enlightenment of NDC members and Democratic voters generally. Now, in the NDC chairman's luxuriously furnished living room, before the sometimes-active NDC executive committee, he was being asked to defend his actions. In fact, to defend his entire strategy in directing the state's NDC.

"You know, maybe he's right, John," another member timidly spoke up. "Vietnam doesn't seem to be quite the fiery issue it was. Maybe we ought to change our emphasis from the War to something else. You don't want to be left swimming upstream all alone."

John, who normally did his best to contain personal opinion and feeling at these meetings, seemed to swell with anger at those remarks. He had hoped someone in the room would remind the others that young men, both American and Vietnamese, were still dying over there; that American planes were dropping more tons of bombs and toxic chemicals than in any other war, and that the obscenity and immorality of that distant conflict were still corroding the fabric of our own society. John finally lashed out. "You may want to work for Henry Jackson or Hubert Humphrey or George Wallace, but I never will. For five years I've fought against this War, devoted my resources and organized others resources trying every approach, working step by step, but always with one overriding goal in mind - to end the War. That was the genesis of NDC, of the Open Primary Bill and now of the delegate challenge. I'm not about to give up that issue for a charismatic personality or some soap-box promises of more money in your pocket. Until the War is really ended, it is the issue and I for one will never work for any candidate who ignores it."

The room had come awake. The strength and obvious sincerity of John's retort had left the other speakers stunned and silent. Somebody spoke a few innocuous words like "yes, that's right," or "let's continue this later;" just enough to break the surface tension set up by John's honesty. Under the camouflage of the room's new movement, a couple members stood up, others stretched and the meeting broke up with the usual hand-shakes, goodbyes and lingering one-to-one conversations.

SUMMER STAFF

Graduation from Brown occurred on schedule. I was faced with several options. However, because the job market for '71 graduates was very tight, fewer options than I would have wished. A university administrator with whom I had become good friends, offered me a rent-free home for the summer, a one-room, chestnut beam cabin which he had reconstructed on the edge of a large organic garden behind his country home. So I decided to remain in Rhode Island for the summer, living in the rustic, yet adequate, cabin in North Kingstown. When Nelson learned this, he asked that I join him and Andy on the NDC summer staff. At a salary of sixty dollars a week, I couldn't resist. It would be a crucial summer for NDC. With the Open Primary Bill all but dead, the brunt of the NDC effort would be locating and preparing delegates for the primary election and Convention challenge. Organizing the middle class proved nothing less than a herculean task.

REVIVAL MEETING

July 7
      To kick off the summer delegate selection campaign we prepared a statewide NDC membership meeting.

99

It was held in the hundred-seat faculty dining center at Rhode Island College. One of our executive committe members, a professor at RIC, had given a very liberal interpretation to the proper use rules of college facilities and reserved it, free of charge, for NDC. This was a liability in one sense. Fearful that a hostile state legislator might object to this political use of state facilities and take it out on the college budget, we, at the last moment, destroyed more than one hundred typed invitations to state senators and representatives. We didn't dare tell Bunny, the housewife volunteer who had spent three days typing the legislators' invitations, of our eleventh hour loss of courage.

The meeting got off to an excellent start. It was nearly a full house with those in attendance very representative of the state's middle-class voters; no chanting students or loud-mouth welfare recipients interrupted our meeting. At the speakers' table sat Nelson. Close by was Syd, back in Providence for this event before beginning a summer in Europe. Beside them were Jack Indeck, serving as master of ceremonies, John Lincoln, an active state NDC member, and the two special guest speakers - Ted Baldwin, one of the campaign organizers behind Duffey's surprising success in Connecticut; and Jerome Grossman, chairman of the Massachusetts Peace Action, Mass Pax.

Indeck, a fortyish, slender, black-haired businessman, started the meeting. He stood at the microphone, his hands gripping the lectern, speaking nervously at first, then slipping into informality, even telling an on-the-way-to-the-Forum story. The chairmanship of NDC was basically no more than a titular position. Though Indeck lent his name to the stationery, he really did not have a working grasp of what Nelson's staff was doing. Even the staff wasn't sure at times.

So when he began explaining the admittedly intricate mechanics of the Primary Bill, delegate selection and challenge options, he transferred his confusion to the audience. Fortunately, it was all very brief and he moved on to introduce the speakers.

First came Sydney, looking very school-girlish in a simple woolen jumper. She spoke in her usual soft, though firm, tone explaining how she had become involved in Rhode Island politics, emphasizing the importance of NDC projects and concluding with a low-keyed, though very effective, plea for money. On cue, near the end of her talk, Andy and I, who had been hovering in the rear of the room, swept into the aisles like church ushers, distributing NDC pledge books. Elmer Gantry couldn't have timed it better and our "revival" meeting had just begun.

Next came the political pro, Ted Baldwin, to explain the success of his organization, Caucus of Connecticut Democrats, and their candidate, Joseph Duffey. It was the story of David and Goliath all over, beautifully told by a well-disciplined speaker. Baldwin concluded by extolling the Rhode Island liberals to keep going - "In politics there are no losers, just quitters."

Grossman followed Baldwin, his deep, strong voice awakening any in the audience who might have drifted off. He didn't speak of winners, losers or policy. He spoke only of power, pure and simple, a political term most in the audience thought was the monopoly of the Blacks and the Gay. They applauded when Grossman said they, the liberal middle class, had goals and aspirations also, that they could flex muscles and exert pressure as well as any other group. Grossman, like most other liberal spokesmen, was a salesman. But, whereas most were selling Edsels, Grossman was selling Cadillacs.

I had heard him talk privately about the mechanics of middle-class politics. He understood that you don't excite the middle class over increased social security benefits or repairing that stoplight on the corner. Middle-class liberals live on "prestige and honor," he said. "To move them you must be dramatic. Don't just say the war in Vietnam is a bad foreign policy, call it the most outrageous, deplorable moment in American history, the greatest crisis since the Revolution. And as far as the Presidential primary, if you want them to donate money, to lobby, to work, you have to offer them the plum of possibly being National Convention delegates themselves, of seeing their names in the paper, talked about by Walter Cronkite and remembered for all posterity in the annals of TIME magazine." Grossman sat down to loud applause. He had excited the audience with promises of power and a brighter self-image. With any luck, that excitement would transfer itself into bigger monthly pledges to pay our salary.

Toward the end, the meeting began to slip into all too familiar liberal befuddlement. John Lincoln, a handsome, curly-haired, retired naval officer, came to the lectern, a mammoth cigar to the side of his mouth. Lincoln and his attractive wife had been loyal to NDC. They had worked hard canvassing their district during the previous summer's state committee elections, and promised support for the upcoming projects. Nelson no doubt was offering him some kind of a plum by putting him on the speakers' list hoping to shore up his commitment to the Coalition. Puffing on his cigar he strayed from discussing the delegate project, stepping into a diatribe against Providence's Mayor Doorley, the state's uncontested Democratic political boss. "Doorley's gang," as Lincoln put it, has got to be stopped. As he went on painting Doorley as a patronage-wielding, opposition-stomping tyrant, in ruthlessness second only to Boss Daley, one got the fanciful impression that this vendetta against the political machine was about to erupt into gang warfare between the regulars and NDC. Nelson jumped to his feet, butting in to ask for questions from the audience.

Then, the three NDC leaders, Indeck, Lincoln and Nelson, stood shoulder to shoulder at the microphone, fielding a barrage of audience questions. Indeck got excited, stating that he'd probably end up in a concentration camp if Nixon appointed one more Supreme Court Justice. Lincoln continued to hammer at Doorley. And Nelson , feeling control slipping quickly, strove vainly to get the discussion back to NDC matters. It all ended about nine-thirty , the heart of Rhode Island's newly inspired liberals returning home to Dick Cavett leaving a messy conference room for Andy and me to clean up.

ELECTORAL PROFILE PROJECT

July 9

It was hotter than hell in Nelson's third floor apartment. The summer's first heat wave had settled over Providence raising the temperature to ninety outside and higher than that in the poorly ventilated apartment. The stagnant air smelled of last night's spaghetti dinner and this morning's tuna Kitty Chow. Andy, who had moved into Nelson's apartment the week before, hung over a kitchen chair like a wet towel, his tortured face staring into a clanking, tabletop fan. Pooh Bear, the black cat, was perched in the window above a sinkful of dirty dishes, swatting at a fly trapped between the rusting screen and grease-caked windowpane. I had no sooner stepped into this macabre scene than I turned to leave. But John, who was working in the office, heard me at the door and called me in.

He was on his knees, barefoot, wearing a yellowed t-shirt and faded blue gym trunks. Reaching under the plywood desk, he was rumaging through the cardboard box which served as his file cabinet. "Hey, look what I found." He climbed back to his feet holding a manila folder with several sheets inside. "Almost forgotten about this."

"What's that?"

"Last year the state Democratic party held a big fund raising dinner. We wanted to know who attended those things; they don't normally list their contributors in the PROVIDENCE JOURNAL." A smile crept across John's face. "So Syd and Andy snuck out there, hiding behind the bushes out front. With binoculars they collected this list of license plate numbers. The terrible thing was that about halfway through it began pouring rain, but they kept at it." John squatted down again to put the file back in the box. "Now all we have to do is compare this to a statewide vehicle registration list."

Hopefully, I thought, that project was not in the offing.

"But that can wait, I guess," John said. "Right now we've got a more important task facing us. " He proceeded to explain the Electorate Profile Program.

EPP was another Nelson brainstorm. John had followed many campaigns and knew exactly what the ingredients of a successful one must be. Knowledge of the electorate was an essential element; having a finger on the individual voters, knowing which ones to call the day of elections to bring out a big vote, which voters to avoid because they can't or won't be of any help, and locating the borderline cases who need the extra push of a persuasive phone call or personal mailing. Facts are prerequisite to power, both acquiring and retaining. Most campaigns wait until the last minute to compile this information, madly dashing through voting lists, phone books and party rolls trying to put facts in order. By starting six months before the proposed state delegate convention, Nelson hoped to avoid this normal eleventh hour confusion.

Furthermore, and perhaps more importantly, I think John imagined EPP would serve as an organizational adhesive within NDC. We had entered the summer's political doldrums. The membership could no longer be called upon to lobby for the Open Primary Bill and the possible challenge convention and primary election was still too distant to excite the loosely aligned members. John felt NDC needed a work project of some sort to put wind in our sails. By having members gather facts and make phone calls, he hoped to keep them in tune or at least thoughtful of more urgent, upcoming activities. Those more critical of, or less sensitive to, such organizational needs might call this busy work.

John explained the details of EPP assigning to me the task of composing and typing an instruction sheet for volunteers. The mechanics of EPP were simple enough for even our slowest of members yet they had enough color to generate interest. The EPP volunteer would first go to his local board of canvassers. Every city hall in the state housed a board of canvassers which holds and updates the voter registration files. There, the volunteer would first purchase the 1970 General Election Voting List covering one voting district, then compare the 1970 voting list to the registration cards in the current files, updating the purchased list. The cards tell when the registrant last voted and, if in a primary, whether Democratic or Republican. Using colored pencils, the EPP volunteer marks to the left of the registrant's name on the purchased list the date he last voted in a primary and which one, using red pencil for Democratic and blue for Republican.

Then, in preparation for telephoning, the volunteer transfers the names from the list to color coded index cards, red for those who voted in the '70 Democratic primary and therefore, due to the twenty-six month rule, could vote only in the Democratic primary in '72; blue for those who voted in the Republican primary; and white for those who voted in neither and were therefore eligible to vote in either Democratic or Republican primary in '72.

Next came the part most volunteers, even the most faithful, hated - telephoning. However, other than door-to-door canvassing, which most people disliked even more, telephoning was the only way to gather the desired information. To make it a little easier and to eliminate those stuttering, inefficient I-forgot-what-I-was-going-to-say phone calls, we composed a questionnaire guide for the telephone canvassers to follow. Though we emphasized that it was merely a memory tool and not to be read verbatim over the phone, I suspect that more than one intimidated telephoner recited it as faithfully as a tape recording of Nixon's inaugural address:

Hello. My name is _____ and I'm a volunteer for the New Democratic Coalition's Voter Information Service. As you probably know, you will have the opportunity next April to vote in Rhode Island's first presidential primary. At that time you will be able to vote for either a Democrat presidential candidate or a Republican presidential candidate, but not both. If you are thinking of voting in the Democratic presidential primary, we have statements and speeches by all the

Democratic candidates which we can mail to you if you'd like to know more about them.
Q#1 - Do you think you will be voting in the Democratic primary? So that you won't have so much material to read all at one time, we'd like to send you speeches on just two issues.
Q#2 - What two issues would you like us to send?
Q#3 - By the way, do you know of any young people who will be eighteen by March 11 who are not yet registered to vote?

From the beginning, I did not like the idea of EPP. It seemed like the type of project best reserved to an organization with an overflow staff or access to a computer and programmer. But John was insistent, so I played my part faithfully.

July 10
My first move was to the Providence City Hall. Deep in the basement within cement and steel vaults, the board of canvassers held the city voter registration lists. Theoretically, these lists were open to the public, but as any political science student who has worked in government will tell you, in politics, rules and practice are not necessarily synonymous - everything is open to interpretation. This is especially true in city politics, particularly Providence city politics.
Those in City Hall who have been assigned the important task of safeguarding the voter registration lists take their job quite seriously. They develop an almost parental attentiveness for the lists. They know that in a democracy it is these lists, their wards, from which all power arises. They know this because their superiors, the elected officials who have appointed them keepers of the lists, have told them so and have

warned that all city jobs, even their own, are only as safe as those lists. Understandably, the keepers are protective, even over-protective of their wards, guarding not only against danger of fire, water and sun, but against the less tangible, though real, threat of intruding political dissidents who would dare to steal their power; or nosy reporters who might dare to suggest that more than one of their wards had recently found notoriety on the obituary page.

As a staff member of the NDC, I clearly constituted the former threat - a political dissident. To have declared myself as such in the marble-pillared switchbox of the city machine would probably have prevented me from examining the registration lists. Then what would I have done? Written a nasty note to the mayor? Applied for redress through the courts? Would the ACLU, busy defending Angela Davis, Dave Dellinger and Daniel Ellsberg, have taken the case of an out-of-state summer political staff worker who was denied access to the board of canvassers office because he had mud on his shoes or garlic on his breath?

So instead of risking failure I employed a common, though seldom admitted political expedient - I lied. When the receptionist-secretary at the board of canvassers asked what I wanted, I explained that I was a student, from Brown, always a useful cover for foolish activity. I spun my yarn saying that I was conducting an independent research project for a political science course. I threw out a couple academic phrases like demographic distribution, statistical correlation, then stated I would need to copy some information from the voter registration files - "assuming that's permissible, I sure don't want to fail the course."

The secretary, a very pleasant lady, was more

than willing to oblige, directing me to a long library
table in the middle of the office where I could copy
whatever information I needed from whichever books
I requested. I began to have second thoughts about the
necessity of my long winded fabrication. It all seemed
quite easy. However, on the way to the table, before
the secretary entered the vault, we encountered
Gaetano Langi, the man in charge.

Langi had the look of a patronage regular entering
his third decade in City Hall. He wore blue-grey
slacks, a bright blue shirt with contrasting tie and
had curly, barbered hair with a hairline decidedly at
ebb tide. As I entered the office he stared suspiciously
over the glass partition around his desk then stepped
out interrupting me as I was about to take a seat at the
table. The secretary, sensing she might have done
something wrong, repeated to Langi what I had told
her, her version sounding more believable than mine.
Langi looked me up and down carefully, taking silent
note of the splice knots in my shoe strings and ink
stains on my frayed work shirt. Pretending he hadn't
heard the secretary's version, he asked why I wanted
to see the registration list. With a sheepish grin, I
retold the story ending with "but our professor said
voters' lists are public documents. Isn't that true?"
Langi, still suspicious, told the secretary to get the
books I asked for, one at a time. He turned to me
saying he hoped it wouldn't take long. I replied that
I hoped it wouldn't take long myself.

Regretably it took longer than I expected. From
noon until three-thirty I poured over the lists of one
voting district marking with red pencil, then blue,
crossing out the deceased or moved, adding the newly
registered. It was a very tedious task. I knew I was
in for a hard time trying to locate and train volunteers
from among the summer-struck NDC membership.

SEARCH FOR VOLUNTEERS

July 11

I began my search for EPP volunteers in Providence using the overworked list of those who had helped in the past. It wasn't a long list. After six phone calls I was already halfway through it without having received a single commitment. The excuses were the usual – "leaving on vacation next week"; "all the children have whooping cough" ; "in the process of remodelling the house." One gruff voiced lady whose bath I had apparently disturbed, suggested I stick the E-P-P up my a-s-s, then hung up. I crossed her name off the list.

The first positive response I received was from Mrs. O, number seven on the list. We kept an index card profile on each member recording not only dues payments but dates contacted, activities and so on. According to the card, Mrs. O had been active from time to time, had attended a couple of meetings last summer, was not presently paying monthly dues but had come to the RIC meeting. On the telephone she was very cordial, said she thought "the nice young people on the NDC staff" were doing a wonderful thing, knew they weren't getting paid much and hoped people appreciated their efforts. Somehow, we got off the EPP topic. She said her husband was barbecuing some hamburgers for lunch and I was welcome to join them. I declined at first, for the simple reason that I didn't like barbecued hamburger. Then Nelson stepped into the office shooting a how's-it-going smile at me. He came up to the desk where I was phoning, looking over my shoulder at the almost depleted volunteer list. I leaned forward,quickly covering the list with an elbow. "I take that back, Mrs. O, " I said. "Sure, I'd enjoy coming over. See you in half an hour. "

I was soon sorry that I had changed my mind.
Mrs. O and her husband were a very considerate
couple. They had a son my age traveling somewhere
they said. I ate the charcoal-grilled hamburger while
explaining the EPP project in detail to Mrs. O. She
listened but said quite firmly that she was opposed
to the idea of telephone canvassing and would not do
it herself. She had begun years ago in the area telephoning during a school board election. She didn't
believe it made any difference and worse, she suspected
it offended some people, including herself, to receive
these phone calls. So that was that. Having consumed
the afternoon unsuccessfully, I thanked them for lunch,
returned to the office and immediately vomitted one
and one half pounds of charcoal broiled hamburger
into Nelson's kitchen sink.

July 12
    The next day I tried again. This time I contacted
a less seasoned political volunteer - Bunny. Bunny
was in her early thirties, the very girlish wife of a
succeeding local professional. Her major volunteer
contribution to that time according to the office profile card, was the typing of one hundred invitations to
the RIC meeting; the ones we quietly disposed of rather
than risk an unfavorable response from a state legislator on the use of state college facilities. Bunny was
very proud of those invitations. She wasn't much of
a typist and it had taken her three days to complete
them. She had folded them too. As I spoke with her
on the phone she said she had worried ever since that
they were folded incorrectly. I assured her that they
had been typed and folded quite professionally, as well
as Teddy Kennedy's personal secretary could have done.
Bunny appreciated that.
    She was one of the liberally educated housewives

who , upon seeing her babies enter the other world of kindergarten and first grade, felt deserted and isolated in her own house. Having married in college, she had no profession to return to, and working part-time at the neighborhood dry cleaners was unacceptably below the dignity of her husband's social standing. So, nudged by desparation, she directed her energies to the drain pipe of volunteer work finding, through a series of chance acquaintances and seasonal probability, the New Democratic Coalition of Rhode Island.

I arrived at Bunny's house within twenty minutes of her offer to help with the Electorate Profile Program. Hers was a moderately expensive home in a neighborhood of well-manicured lawns on the East Side of Providence. Petite, Bunny had a little girl cuteness about her. At the door she exhibited a childish shyness, blushing when I introduced myself and asked to come in. But once we sat together in a few minutes of conversation, she became herself, flushing now with a surprising enthusiasm and interest in liberal politics. She wanted to know about NDC. "At parties I'm always getting into debates on politics but it's always the others who have all the facts," she pouted. "I feel so defeated." I explained the history of the national NDC and the Rhode Island organization, spicing it up by dropping as many big names as I could remember. McGovern and Kennedy she recognized; the rest went right over her head.

Before I could get into explaining about the blue and red pencils of the EPP, Bunny insisted upon showing me a copy of her brother's undergraduate thesis on the Electoral College. It was suffering from jaundiced pages. He had written it in 1957. I promised to send her whatever information we could glean from the CONGRESSIONAL RECORD on the Electoral College. Finally, I began my uninterrupted spiel on EPP pulling out the voting list I had prepared at the Providence

112

board of canvassers. Bunny warned that she wasn't very good on the phone; that, as a matter of fact, such calls to strangers frightened her. But for a good cause she would try nonetheless. I reassured her that NDC was indeed a good cause and then suggested that she call only those names in the first column of the voting list and I would call those in the second column. In a week or so we would get together again, I promised, compare results and discuss strategy. Bunny was a-menable to that. In fact, she preferred the idea of being as much under NDC staff direction as possible. She worked best, she told me, when she didn't have to make decisions. EPP was the project for her.

STAFF MEETING

July 15
    As a staff, John, Andy and I gradually solidified. There were some problems at first. The usual hair length controversy quickly resolved by Andy and I getting haircuts thus placating Nelson's more conservative views. My living on a farm in North Kingstown also created occasional problems. Commuting for one. It took forty minutes to drive into Providence. On occasion, my notoriously undependable '62 Oldsmobile didn't make it, usually on the nights of important district meetings. John and Andy would gladly have made room for me in the Orms Street office-apartment, then I would have been prompt for all meetings, available twenty-four hours a day for last minute mimeographing and able to attend to recalcitrant members at first call. However, in my simple North Kingstown cabin, I had birds to wake me in the morning, fresh air to revive me after long meetings, a bountiful organic garden and one dozen laying hens. I refused to

exchange that tranquility, stability and economic independence for the urban convenience of Orms Street. By mid-July, the correctness of that decision was apparent.

John called Andy and I into the office. It was a typical staff meeting. John, his white t-shirt outlining a lean, nearly gaunt torso, sat against the edge of the plywood counter. He was always smiling at staff meetings, exuding enthusiasm and exuberance, hoping, as the organizational management texts promised, it would be contagious. After the first couple of meetings however, Andy and I developed an immunity.

John began by laying plans for the coming weeks. Our summer objective was to conduct a series of district organization meetings across the state finding a chairman for each district. Beginning with the list of RIC meeting attendees, we would have to telephone people in each area and locate first, a house for each meeting and, second, people to attend. Our first district meeting was to be in Providence.

"Who wants to make the calls for this week's meeting?" John asked hopefully. With notebook and pen in my lap, I continued to scribble notes of John's earlier statements, not daring to look up. Andy, pulling heavily on a cigarette, stared blindly out the window. For a full minute there was complete silence. My head remained bowed, Andy froze in his empty stare and Nelson maintained his eager smile. It was a common scene. Finally, Andy sighed and gave in raising his hand lethargically. Nelson's eyebrows jumped halfway up his forehead and his smile widened to an impish grin. "That's great Andy. Thanks." He jotted it down on his clipboard while I raised my head, shaking off the sand.

"Now for the bad news," John announced theatrically. "It appears we, that is NDC, is bankrupt."

"Again?" Andy interjected.

114

"Yes, as of today, the balance in our account is zero. To pay the five hundred dollar deficit which we'll incur as we go through these last two weeks of July we'll have to use the anticipated August dues money. That, of course, means that if we're to continue, we'll have to double the August budget." John spoke with the incomprehensible clarity of an accountant. What he was telling us was that we would not be receiving our salary checks that week, or next. The fall was considerably shortened, however, by an earlier cut in our salary from sixty dollars a week to thirty.

"What we'll have to do now," John continued, "is work twice as hard to get more donations coming in next month. We'll have to get more pledge books out, be more consistent and thorough in our follow-up calls and increase the pace of our district organizational meetings and coffee hours." A squirrel on a treadmill with a carrot dangling before it could not have been in a worse situation. John had been working very efficiently under these near starvation conditions for years. I think now he hoped they would prove an incentive to his staff also. Fortunately, I had a very adequate supply of carrots; organic carrots at that.

LUNCH WITH EVANS

July 20
I arrived at Orms Street in midafternoon after lunch with Dave Evans of Governor Licht's staff. Dave had mentioned about a week earlier that he wanted to get together with me; I supposed to examine and weigh a new political entity. I was too busy at the time to set a definate date. But while making district meeting calls I spoke with him again at which time he suggested we lunch together that day. I agreed.

At noon I drove to the capitol. Dave's office was in the State House adjacent to the Governor's office. Actually, he and Rick Jerue, another young staff member, shared a cramped desk space in the far corner of the Governor's suite. It was a puny allotment compared to Licht's plush, black leather swivel chair and wide mahogany desk. There were some visitors, a young Rhode Island family, walking through the Governor's office, mouths agape, impressed by the furniture-wax facade.

Dave was an articulate, well-spoken political Lord Fauntleroy. Approaching thirty, balding with a shaggy halo of hair, chubby from lack of exercise ("I'm trying to stay away from bread.") and prone to smoke a good deal, he was very much a young political favorite. He dressed modishly and wore round-framed, horn-rimmed sunglasses. I had heard Dave's name spoken frequently by Nelson and met him for the first time during an Alternatives For Social Change seminar at Brown a few months earlier. I had heard him speak again at an NDC executive committee meeting in the spring. Those brief encounters had impressed me – not only did he speak well and intelligently, but he had a grasp of political realities which went far beyond that of most NDC members or student activists.

He suggested we go to William's in Wayland Square, a fashionable businessman's and rich woman shopper's lunch stop. I countered with, "How about Walden Center?"

"Oh, that health food place?"

"Well, yes. It's a macrobiotic restaurant."

"Fine, let's do that," he accepted reluctantly. "It will be quite a lark."

"I eat there all the time."

We stopped off at his apartment first. It was on The Hill in the better, or at least the wealthier, part of town. His was a modern apartment, no doubt expensive, with sliding patio doors, plush carpet, coordinated furnishings in contemporary plastic decor, and in the center of the living room floor a large, royal blue shag rug with "McCarthy" embroidered on it. An aging female spaniel had greeted us at the door. Dave knelt down to fondle and caress her, speaking affectionately. When he left the room for a minute she sniffed me indignantly and scooted on her butt across the McCarthy rug.

"Nice place you have here."

"Oh, thanks."

I could not help comparing the plastic glitter luxury of this apartment to John Nelson's hole in the wall on Orms Street.

Walden Center was a bit too much for the unitiated Dave. We had the usual fare - miso soup, mung bean salad, boiled seaweed, squash sauteed in wheat germ oil, and carrot juice. It was a full house, so we ate at the long, bench-table in the center of the minsicule restaurant. The slender, middle-aged, Czechoslovakian guru proprietor was sitting in a booth opposite us with assorted friends - a frizzy-bearded hippy in flannel shirt and jeans, and a dirty-faced, flat-nosed girl with stringy blonde hair that fell forward into her soybean casserole. On our other side was a dark-eyed mother, buxom and unbloused, holding her nursing baby in her arms. The baby was not pacified, however. It screamed mercilessly making Dave's continuous political talk difficult to hear, let alone digest.

Dave obviously had a point he wanted to make that afternoon. He didn't like Nelson's challenge strategy. He would prefer to see NDC follow the Licht primary route. Dave was not only on Licht's staff, but the undeclared, yet indisputable director of McGovern's unofficial Rhode Island campaign effort.

117

"The possibility of a successful delegate challenge is, quite candidly, Bruce, very remote." That news hardly shocked me. He went on: "The due effort clause in the McGovern Rules is the escape clause for the regular delegates in Rhode Island and they know it. On paper it looks like Hogan and Bevilacqua did everything they could to get reform enacted. To the whole world it looks like the bill was defeated by those wanting proportionality, more radical reform, as well as those wanting no reform. His statements implied that this was the strategy of the anti-reform elements all along. Dave was an astute observer who had been playing in Rhode Island politics long enough to read the handwriting on the wall. But his statements to me were more than just astute observations. Unstated, but obviously, he wanted this message conveyed to Nelson.

The baby's crying was getting to Dave about this time. He lit another cigarette and looked distainfully around him, wishing, no doubt, that he was having lunch within the serenity of William's, alone. I suggested he attend our next district meeting and bring up his argument against the challenge there. He said no, he was fearful of people accepting him as no more than a spokesman for the Governor's office. "Even Harold Arcaro won't accept me as my own man," he complained. Dave had to be back in the office by one, so we regrettably ended our conversation prematurely. As we left Walden Center, the baby wailing behind us, I had the feeling that we would not be having lunch together again.

PROVIDENCE MEETING

July 24

    To get an attendance of twelve people at our district
meetings, we had to contact as many as sixty people;
not just any sixty names out of the phone book, but
names from our lists of self-declared liberals who had
attended meetings in the past, worked in political campaigns or made donations to our cause. The three of
us would sit in the office, each at his own telephone,
calling number after number, explaining, chiding,
pleading, until our ears were red and cauliflowered.

    In making my share of the Providence meeting
calls, I had phoned Bunny. Her voice hesitated after
I identified myself. "Oh, I've been a bad girl," she
whimpered.

    "How's that?" I said.

    "I didn't make my phone calls." For a moment
I didn't know what she was talking about.

    "Oh, your EPP phone calls you mean." In the
planning of district meetings and a new donation drive,
I had put EPP on the bottom of the schedule, forgetting
to make my phone calls also. I assuaged Bunny's
guilt feelings assuring her we would have plenty of
time to complete that project before the results were
needed. But as part of her self-imposed penance,
she volunteered her house for the Providence district
meeting.

    "You can have the house for the meeting as long
as I don't have to take a big part in it," she said.
"I'm not a leader at all and I could never act as chairman or anything like that." I immediately accepted
her offer then continued searching for attendees.

    The highest concentration of the state's established
liberals was in Providence. That, however, did not

mean it was easy organizing meetings there. What
the Providence liberals made up for in numbers, they
lacked in quality. One call to a Mrs. P was particularly depressing. Her voice was gravelly and, at
times, quite sharp. She was an old ADA organizer
back in the Stevenson days when being a liberal was
a dangerous, though respectable occupation. Her
old fears showed through when she complained about
my picture-taking at the RIC meeting: "I don't suppose the FBI will confiscate your files," she spoke
indignantly. "If they were really concerned with your
group, they would have had someone there that night
taking his own pictures." She gave me a long-winded,
rambling lecture on the right to privacy. Finally, I
was able to interrupt long enough to explain our summer delegate selection project and urge her to attend
the Providence meeting. "Oh, I don't see the use
really," she went on. "You know, my husband and
I have been at this a long time now and it doesn't make
one iota's difference. We're jostling at windmills."
Regrettably, I convinced Mrs. P to attend the meeting.
Her comments became a self-fulfilling prophecy.

The Providence district meeting, for all our calling,
recalling and preparation, was a miserable debacle
of intellectual, liberal defeatism.   Mr. and Mrs. P,
billing themselves as "connoisseurs of lost causes,"
led off the disaster: "You know, we've been around
for a long time," Mrs. P told the dozen people assembled in Bunny's living room. "Mr. P was in the as-
sessor's office for years. We've seen first hand the
need for reform and don't think we haven't tried."
Mrs. P gave a self-satisfied smile and nod to Mr. P
beside her. "Organizations like your NDC are needed,
of course, but I think after you've lived a little longer,"
(John and I were the only persons under thirty in the
room), "you'll see that things really aren't so bad after

all; that all your excitement and work was just an exercise in futility. Why bother?"

A wild-eyed, balding university science professor was next to deliver a blow to our frail organization. Professor L was in his mid-thirties, a loud and childishly demanding character. "Why bother indeed," he yelled across the room, "and if you are going to bother, then why bother with such a futile plan as a state delegate challenge convention." He was lecturing, not discussing. "Anyone who has been in this state for more than a day," he sideglanced John and I, "can see clearly that the probability of a successful challenge hovers near zero." Without having heard Nelson's complete explanation of the present Presidential primary strategy, Professor L hammered away at the "technical infeasibility" of a challenge in the state. Factually, we had not yet decided on which course of action to pursue, a challenge delegation or a slate of proportionally committed delegates on the primary ballot. All the facts were not yet in. For all his scientific, analytic jargon, Professor L seemed little concerned with the facts or the truth. He filibustered for another half-hour. Those six or seven attendees who over the phone had expressed a genuine interest in the project, were so discouraged and confused by this unabatable attack, that most finally retreated into staring at their watches.

The meeting wandered, foundered, then finally collapsed. Mr. and Mrs. P and Professor L were the first to leave. Though they had insisted upon assuming leading roles in the organizational meeting, they were not heard from again - this to the immeasurable benefit of those serious about political reform.

EAST GREENWICH MEETING

Organizing in southern Rhode Island was a horse or a different color; sadly, though, just as stubborn. Our first meeting there was in the East Greenwich home of Mr. and Mrs. Lincoln. Theirs was a comfortable home in an area of open fields and woods. Beyond their wide lawn, they maintained a fertile organic garden crowded with a midsummer's crop of green beans, cucumbers, kale and green peppers.

John, Andy and I, driving down from Providence, arrived a little late for the seven o'clock meeting. Nelson took a seat near the center of the living room on a richly overstuffed burgundy sofa. Andy and I sat on the floor, the remainder of the chairs in the room having been taken by the dozen attendees. There were new faces at this meeting, people who hadn't been involved in the state anti-War movement or the past summer's Democratic committee election. The Lincoln's were in an area where it was difficult to find liberal Democrats. Yet, with the same steadfastness they had shown in earlier NDC projects, they located and pulled in these people with little more to promise them than another political presentation and a cup of coffee.

Nelson began by speaking of the primary election law reform bill emanating from the Hogan Commission and introduced in the legislature by Rep. Bevilacqua. It did not call for the sweeping reforms of the Open Primary Bill, yet it was a step better than the law on the books at that moment. An attempt to tack on an amendment for proportionality had been defeated in a Democratic caucus. Nelson added that he had just received a phone call from Sen. Michaelson informing him that the Bevilacqua bill would not reach the Senate floor that year, that there were not even enough votes to get it out of committee. Michaelson believed some Presidential primary reform bill would be passed when the legislature began their new session in January, but as to the scope of its reform, he could not even guess. He warned Nelson not to expect too much though.

"As I see it now," Nelson offered to the attentive group, "we have two alternatives. We can hold a state Democratic convention and select a group of delegates to challenge the regulars at the National Convention, or we can hold a state Democratic convention to form a counter-slate to put on the primary election ballot. Either way, we have to prepare now for that convention in January and find people willing to serve as delegates for either a challenge or a counter-slate.

That, of course, was what these district meetings were all about - how to organize well enough to conduct a successful state convention in January. That was not easy when it appeared to many people that there was still a possibility of the state legislature passing reforms liberalizing the primary elections, making a challenge or counter-slate unnecessary. This was the strategy of the anti-reform element within the Rhode Island Democratic party, i.e., let the liberals rest securely in false hopes.

Sen. Callaghan, co-sponsor of S-272, had also been in touch with Nelson. He had told John that at the Democratic caucus which had effectively killed the Bevilacqua bill for that session, the only senator to speak against it was Joe Rodgers of District 10, while he, Arcaro and Leary had spoken in its favor. Callaghan believed that the rest of the legislators did not understand what the hell was happening. They had no idea what all this reform business was about. No

one had even brought up the topic of the McGovern
Commission guidelines. Yet, they were easily intimidated by Mayor Joe Doorley's power and everyone knew that Sen. Joe Rodgers was patronage-boss
Doorley's senate trouble shooter. Callaghan felt
the only way to get a reform bill through the legislature was to get Doorley to call off Sen Rodgers. The
bill, he felt, would pass easily then. He warned
Nelson that an early announcement of a challenge
convention would "get their hackles up," and further
reduce the chance of passing reform legislation in
January.

It was again Nelson's move. He understood the
stakes well enough to know that Doorley and the entrenched party regulars were not about to relinquish
one centimeter of territory. If they could block reform and still be seated at the National Convention,
they would do just that. There was no point in waiting
for them to write the reform legislation. John's decision was to pursue the challenge convention without
hesitation and it was for support that he turned to the
attendees of the East Greenwich meeting.

He concluded his presentation by directing a simple
question to the small group: "How can we have a voice
in Rhode Island politics, effectively organize the people
and get our delegates to the National Convention?" His
question was met by silence. Then the Lincolns came
through again. Mrs. Lincoln offered her availability
for staff work and Mr. Lincoln accepted the call to
serve as district chairman. Then, with the confidence
that most of our members lacked, he pointed to a friend
sitting beside him and said, "And you can be the chairman in your district."

LOWER CLASS POLITICS

July 29

If our NDC middle-class clientele were only as simple and easily aroused as the lower classes, organizing would have been an easier matter. Saul Alinsky was the great student and chronicler of organizing the blue-collar community. I carried around a dog-eared copy of his REVEILLE FOR RADICALS, constantly seeking clues to the motivating and organizing of our NDC liberals.

In Providence there was an Alinsky-style community organizing group called PACE, run by a genius of that genre, Stan Holt. Holt was a professional radical. As a specialist in block-club organzing, he had been imported into Providence by the Catholic diocese. The deal was this: the diocese placed a large sum (around forty thousand, I had heard)in a trust fund account. Holt was to draw from this account to conduct the business of organizing the residence of a certain area in Providence, turning that disconnected, crime-burdened and apathetic area into a genuine, viable community, much as Alinsky had done with the Woodlawn area of Chicago. Alinsky tactics were always controversial, thus Holt insisted upon the trust fund. It protected his efforts from the censorship of the closely held purse string. His staff consisted of activist students and local people who were willing to work for thirty dollars a week.

Holt had agreed to let me sit in on one of the twice weekly staff meetings which were held in the privacy of the midnight hours (from ten to two) at the PACE store-front office near the corner of Broad and Public Streets. It was a hot, humid night. The sidewalk door was wide open so I stepped in quietly. Holt, dark-haired and lean, stood in front of a small staff huddle, one leg propped on a metal-frame chair. He was taking orders for a run to the local late hour greasy spoon. "Alright, here's what I got written down: two Cokes, one Fanta orange, a coffee white with two lumps, two orders of fries, Fritoes, potato chips and a pack of Kools. That it?" He spoke sharply, like a drill sergeant at roll call. Suddenly taking notice of me, he added, "What about you?"

"What?"

"Food," he came back hard. "Do you want anything from Louie's Greasy Grill?"

"No," I said. "No thanks."

"Here Jimbo," Holt gave the scribbled list to a tall Black man in the huddle, along with a five dollar bill. "We'll divvy up when you get back." Jim slipped out the door.

The PACE office looked like an abandoned military bunker - a cement floor painted navy gray, cinder-block walls, boarded-up display windows and florescent lights flickering overhead. The furnishings were sparse - a couple Salvation Army desks in the corner, two warped fold-up tables pushed against the back wall with an antique Royal typewriter and stacks of miscellaneous printed material, a dented gray file cabinet with a black phone on top, and in the center of the room, serving as the conference table, a junked dining-room table with veneer peeling from the sides and a mismatched center leaf.

Holt and the five remaining staff workers waited for Jim to return before starting the meeting. I stepped around the table to the back desk area. Newspaper clippings covered the wall telling of real estate transactions. Several manila envelopes hung above the phone in a row, like Christmas stockings, each with a staff member's name on it. Above each current

name were several more crossed out, the envelopes
having witnessed many staff turnovers.

One of the staff members had returned to her seat
behind the Royal typewriter. I watched as she finished
typing a brief letter. She was a beautiful girl with
untamed cocoa-brown hair, dark, burning eyes and
a smooth olive complexion. When I smiled at her
she stared at me, then said, "You're from NDC,
aren't you?" I presumed Holt had mentioned I was
coming. I nodded. "That means you're working for
John Nelson?" she went on, holding me in her stare.

Hoping we had struck upon common ground already,
I said confidently, "Yes, of course. John and I work
together on the NDC staff." Moving a little closer I
asked, "Do you know Nelson?"

"Oh yes," she said with a bit of playfulness in
her voice. "We're old enemies."

Back on uncommon ground, I ventured cautiously,
"Major enemies or just little enemies?"

In the low and serious tone of a very certain woman,
"Strong feelings of animosity on my part."

After a few moments pause, I responded in my least
provocative voice, "Oh," then moved on before she
cared to transfer some of that animosity to me. John
explained later that he and this girl, Mac J, had had
several disputes over leadership questions during
student strike days and the Moratorium Day protests.
Mac wanted to radicallize the student anti-War protests, John claimed, and to use the student canvass
volunteers to distribute some "revolutionary" material.
John was not about to let her do that.

Jim returned holding two brown bags of Louie's
Greasy Grill's best. The staff moved in, each taking
out his share. Holt, who had ordered nothing for himself, hit the table twice with the flat of his hand, "Okay,
let's get the meeting started." Jim, the tall, silent

Black, sat down first, unfolding a chair and putting it to the side of the conference table. A skinny, pimply-faced college student, Bruce D, put his chair beside Jim's. Opposite them sat Jack, an odd looking, older fellow in white socks, baggy, gray work pants and a white t-shirt. He was a bean pole, shaped like Derwood Kerby with a long, drawn-out face and swollen chin. To the side and slightly behind Jack, sat a nun. "Sister" something-or-other I heard Holt call her. She wore no habit, just a 1949-length, flannel skirt, frilless white blouse and butterfly-frame glasses mended at the hinge with dirty white adhesive tape. Little more than a heavy bronze cross and chain hanging from her neck set her apart from a million other sadly unattractive spinsters. I sat at the end of the table. Mac, choosing not to join us, merely swiveled in her typewriter chair to face Holt. The sixth member of the staff, Holt's "second lieutenant," Larry G, stood a few feet from Holt, arms crossed, leaning against the frame of the open door.

Holt, standing between the conference table and a washed-out black board, began the staff meeting in the serious, carefully spoken speech of a football coach opening a Monday morning practice. Pacing back and forth, head down, flipping a piece of ivory chalk in one hand while the other jangled coins in his pocket, he examined some of the "team" problems. "Sammy tells me his block club people are really boiling over that intersection. They've been turned down three times for a traffic light. Yesterday, somebody ran over a dog there." Without missing a step, Holt looked up and said, "That's your area, isn't it Jimbo?"

Jim's eyes rolled up and he nodded. Holt continued, "Now's the time to act. The people are mad. You'll get'em to a block club meeting now. It was a dog yes-

128

terday. They're afraid it'll be a little girl tomorrow.
When they're steamed, Jimbo," Holt slammed a fist
into a palm, "bang, that's when you've gotta get'em."
Holt was in his upper thirties, a handsome man with
a boyish, full head of hair and piercing eyes, deep
brown like mahogany. He spoke with the sureness
and rapidity of a courtroom lawyer, shaking his head
vehemently when a staff member got off the track,
usually interrupting with a merciless "Bull shit!"
   "I don't know," Jim drawled back. "Sammy may
be worried, but nobody else cares 'bout that light
till the kids start back to school, anyhow."
   "Bull shit!" Holt shot back stopping dead in his
tracks. "August is here. It's hot, people are miserable, cranky, irritable. Get them angry now and
you'll have that traffic light by September. And when
they have that traffic light, then they'll know how to
get other things when they want to. Then a little girl
won't have to be run down in the street before they
act." Holt paused, "Or even a dog."
   The room was hushed. Jim lowered his head,
nodding. Holt started to return to his pacing but then
stopped, cocked his head upwards, listening. A high
toned electrical buz was coming from above. Holt
stalked it, walking below the nearest light, pulling
the string to turn it off, then listening. The buzzing
was still there. He pulled the string again. The light
flickered back on. Then he stepped under a second
light, pulling its string, again listening. The buzzing
continued. He turned that light back on and walked
to the third light fixture, everyone in the room watching
attentively. He held the string in his hand a moment,
looking around at all of us, then, in a single jerk, he
pulled it, clicking off the light. The buzzing died
instantaneously. He smiled as the staff sighed. After
a moment he realized the room was too dark, so he

pulled the string once again. The light flickered back on. The buzzing returned with it, but Holt took no notice.

"How's that landlord trial coming Jack?" Holt returned to business. Jack had been assigned the task of organizing a mock trial of absentee landlords conducted by the tenants in his block club area - sort of a people's court.

Jack looked down at his notes. "I've got one hundred seventy tenants who   said they'd come for sure and I contacted all twenty-five landlords."

"That's fine, Jack," Holt chuckled. "May even attend that one myself."

Jack looked worried. "I don't know. What if the landlords won't come to their own execution?"

Holt spun around and snapped back, "Then you just phone them and ask whether they'd rather have a hundred shouting, picketing people on their front lawns."

Jack smiled and said, Yeah, that should work. Some of the block people are fit to be tied they're so pissed   about this whole thing. At our meeting last Sunday you shoulda heard the things they were saying about the landlords."

"I hope you took it all down," Holt said.

"Oh, no," Jack blushed. "Most of it was too dirty and I forgot the rest."

Holt looked up to heaven waving his arms in exasperation. "So what!" he screamed. "Make it up! This is important. If you are going to organize these people, you've got to put an enemy in front of them - a well-groomed enemy. Otherwise, everytime you get your community people assembled, the meeting will degenerate to a bull session. To act, you've got to have an enemy."

Next to give his progress report was Bruce D, an anemic, urban studies student at Brown. His was

130

the bread and butter of the Alinsky-organizing strategy - the traffic light. He had organized a block club in the Elmwood district with the issue of getting the city to put in a light at one of those "borderline" intersections. The city traffic division refused the club's request so Bruce D got the neighborhood members to stage a traffic jam protest at the intersection. "Eight cars participated," Bruce D said softly, though proudly.

"How long?" Holt interrogated.

"Oh, at least fifteen minutes, maybe longer," Bruce D replied even softer.

Holt smirked. "Well Brucie, congratulations. Fifteen whole minutes. One quarter of an hour," he taunted. "And I suppose you had them backed all the way to the mayor's office?"

"That's what you gotta do," Larry G broke his silence stepping away from the door to the table. "You gotta get to the mayor. You make Doorley start worrying about that traffic light in Elmwood, then maybe you'll get it."

Bruce D agreed. He presented his plan to "get to the mayor," to find out "where he drinks, what women he stops off to see on his way home." This excited Larry G. He stepped in front of Holt expressing his interest in pursuing this. Holt obligingly sat down.

Larry G was a Bogart-character. Though probably no older than twenty-two, he shuffled back and forth like an old back-room pro, chain smoking Kools. While talking, he would walk over to the black board, light a cigarette then shuffle back to the door, cough, wheeze, then finally pull up a clot of congestion and spit it out on the sidewalk. Looking down at the cigarette, he would then throw the butt out onto the rain slick street, shuffle back to the black board and light another.

131

"Doorley's got a summer home on Beaver Trail,"
he said. "I'm not sure exactly where. They've taken
down all the name signs. But how's this," Larry G
tucked in his shirt, "I'll pose as a delivery man, uni-
form and all, and find out from the neighbors which
house is his. Then we got'em. Right? If he's got a
boat out there, we'll find out where he parks it. He
just ain't about to have no more fun till your people
get their traffic light. Ain't that right?" Larry looked
directly at Bruce D who responded by nodding emphatically.

Holt jumped up again. "What's a matter," he said
looking directly at Bruce D, "cat got your tongue?
You gotta talk or they'll never hear you. It's not like
they're listening." He changed his tone to one of sym-
pathy. "Come on, tell us what you say over the phone
to get the people out for a protest at the intersection.
What do you sound like on the phone?" Bruce D was
uncomfortably on the spot. Holt was a professor teaching
a lesson. "I'll tell you how you sound," Holt went on.
"Like a piece of soggy milquetoast, a stenographer
with sinus trouble." Mimicking in an emotionless
monotone, "Hello, my name is Brucie and I want you
to come to the traffic jam it will be like all the others."
The artistry of Holt's method was irresistable. Everyone laughed, including Bruce D. The lesson was learned
and Holt moved on to the next subject. Finally, at two,
the staff meeting ended and I returned, gladly, to the
problems of organizing the middle class.

AUGUST DROPOUTS

It was the best of months; it was the worst of months; and absolutely nothing in between. Our district meetings continued. Like a band of tinkers, we presented our wares in homes across the state delivering our plan for electoral reform to all who would listen. At times, it seemed no one was listening.

Entering the month, we were seemingly well organized with a definate plan which we enumerated and printed as a small flyer and distributed to members. Our "Action Program" was:

1. Announce that we are preparing to challenge the party's delegation at the '72 Convention with a delegation of our own unless the party complies with the Call to its own Convention.
2. Suggest a way for the party to comply, regardless of legislative inaction again next session through:
   State committee amendment of its by-laws at its coming meeting to prohibit state committee endorsement of delegates.
3. Call upon all Democratic leaders, that is, the Presidential candidates, the chairman of the Democratic National Committee, the Rhode Island Congressional delegation, the national committeeman and -woman, the Governor and the state chairman, to testify in behalf of prohibition of state committee endorsement before the party's subcommittee on by-laws (of which our director is a member).
4. Lobby with state legislators now in their home districts to encourage passage of the NDC Presidential primary next session.
5. Begin immediately to find votes and build an NDC delegation. NDC delegates will be selected at a

state NDC convention in January. The delegation will either be entered in the primary, if the party complies, or it will challenge at the Convention in July.

On the reverse of that flyer, we boasted nine district chairmen, people who were confident enough not only to offer their names, but even dared to list their home phone numbers. By the second week in August, flaws developed in that confidence. Within days the whole structure seemed to be shattering.

First, I received a call from the husband of one of our Providence district chairmen. "I'm awfully sorry," he said, "but my wife is so worried over this. She didn't get any of her calling done. It's just, well, it's just too much for her."

The North Kingstown district chairman called next. He chatted about the latest newspaper article on NDC, then the weather. Finally saying, "You know, I've been thinking. Maybe you'd better find someone else to be chairman here, somebody with more time." He spit it out quickly as if expecting a reprimand. "Oh, it's not like I don't think NDC is doing the right thing. I'm sure you guys are. But with my work and this big house, well, hell, I barely have time to read the Sunday comics."

The following day I called the South Kingstown district chairman. I asked how things were coming along in his district. He replied with a bit of bravado at first; "Oh, don't you boys up in Providence worry about a thing. We're taking care of everything down here." But then as I began to explain a new district chairman assignment, he blurted out, "Hold it!" Now he sounded considerably subdued. "I think I should resign. I don't know anybody down here with an interest in all this reform talk and I don't have the time to go out

searching." Changing his tack slightly; "Besides,
I'm not so sure John is doing the right thing."
Our Barrington district chairman was next to
drop out. We received a letter from her. She wanted
to help and promised to keep paying monthly dues,
but being a district chairman, well, that was just too
great a responsibility. These August casualities, although they were great demoralizers to Andy, John and
I, could have been predicted in July. We had wanted
and felt we needed a grass-roots leadership so des-
parately, that in some cases we created chiefs where
there were only Indians.
But August was also a month of positive organization
building. Rhode Island, like any community, had its
share of active, politically-oriented citizens who were
willing and often anxious to assume leadership responsibility. During the last weeks of our summer campaign, several joined the NDC movement. They came
together with some ideas of their own and the energy to
fulfill Nelson's hope of an operable, decision-making
executive committee.

NATHANS MEETING

August 25
I have made an observation which I call the Political
Halflife Phenomenon. As different individuals entered
our "Little Rhody reform movement," I noted their
length of stay. Some lasted a week, others a month,
some very few seemed to remain in the political arena
eternally, outlasting even the campaigns. Of course,
each and every one of them was wearing down under
the strain, their political interest constantly on the
wane. Some just seemed to wear at a slower rate than
others. Those with the most energy to contribute would

be either those newly initiated into politics or the experienced with a long political halflife. At our August executive committee meeting, we finally hit upon a stable combination.

It was held at the suburban home of Yvette Nathans, a political neophyte, and a gorgeous one. The young wife of a successful dentist, Yvette was the spice our organization had always lacked. She would step into a meeting with all the educated and enticing charm of Mae West, reactivating a flagging discussion, and yet, so subtly, with a Parisian suaveness. Rebecca Fury was another beautiful and very welcome addition to the executive committee. A young mother in Cranston, Rebecca entered our ranks fresh with a very feminine, optimistic excitement. She intended to be a Convention delegate and that was that.

There were other new and welcome faces at the August meeting: Whitney Perkins, a gray-haired, pipe-smoking Brown professor who offered a sense of dignity and establishment to the gathering; Dick Millward, a younger mathmatics professor with a clear, analytic, yet always sanguine approach to NDC problems. Familiar and reliable faces were there too; the Barbours of Bristol, the Lincolns of East Greenwich, Chairman Indeck, plus a smattering of other members from across the state. Finally, I thought as the NDC staff sat back and listened to the others talk, we have a chance for success. Good goals and strategy we had always had; John's creative genius had provided that. Now, it seemed to me, we had at long last found that determining number of leaders to accomplish those goals. That really was what we, the summer '71 staff, had set out to accomplish. True, our June aspirations had exceeded our August attainments, but that we had progressed was unquestionable.

August 29

The NDC summer staff dissolved with neither bang nor whimper. Andy was preparing to return to his parents' Connecticut home for two weeks before starting his senior year at Brown. Though he would remain in touch with Syd, John and the others, he no longer cared to take an active part in NDC. John continued at his post on Orms Street, perhaps freer with two less mouths to feed. He remained the leader of an awakening movement that had miles and miles still to go. I, an unemployed, ivy-league graduate, drifted out of Rhode Island ending up as a seasonal hand on a large organic farm in Pennsylvania where the only organizing I faced was the collards from the kale. But I had not yet turned away from Rhode Island politics. I had participated, nominally, though sincerely, in a significant electoral reform movement. I would be there for the crescendo and climax - the state challenge convention and the Democratic Presidential primary itself.

COME HOME AMERICA

When I had left Rhode Island at the end of August, Nelson, standing in familiar white t-shirt and gym trunks in front of his Orms Street apartment, had shook my hand, offered a grin-and-bare-it smile, then said, "Well, thus ends another summer with nothing to show." That he had underestimated his own efforts was obvious upon my February return to the state. The month before, on January 26, 1972, a new primary bill was signed into law by Governor Licht. Though it retained the twenty-six month rule and the winner-take-all aspect of the Presidential primary, it did bring to fruition some of the reforms NDC had proposed and worked for. Those included the elimination of the Democratic state committee endorsement authority and postponement of the primary date from April 11 to May 23. Under the new rules governing Rhode Island's Presidential primary, delegate slates would be selected at open, public meetings.

STATE DELEGATE CONVENTION

In the beginning of February, it appeared that only one Democratic Presidential candidate would place his name on the ballot - Senator Edmund Muskie. After all, he was the party favorite, everyones "best bet"

138

for the nomination, running high in the national polls
and the native son of New England. Opening the door
for "their man Ed," the leader of the state party regulars Providence Mayor Joseph Doorley, announced
on February 7 a Muskie delegate selection meeting
to be held February 27 at the Biltmore Hotel. He did
so as the state law provided in consultation with a
representative of the Presidential candidate. Muskie's
representative in this case was Joseph Bartlett of
Boston.

Two weeks earlier, Nelson had announced the date
of the NDC-sponsored "State Delegate Convention For
the Proportional Slate" - also February 27. At this
convention, the object of our NDC labor since June,
a slate of delegates would be selected representing all
the Presidential candidates of the Democratic Party
for whom significant support existed in Rhode Island.
The national rules allowed Rhode Island twenty-two
delegate votes. On the proportional slate, the number
of delegates representing each of the Presidential contenders would be determined by balloting at the state
convention prior to the selecting of delegates. If, for
example, 50% of the citizens at the convention voted
for George McGovern, then McGovern would be allowed
50% of the twenty-two delegates on the proportional
slate. The other Presidential candidates would receive
a number of the remaining delegates also in proportion
to their popularity as determined in the balloting. The
delegates themselves would be selected by caucus,
each group which supported a particular Presidential
candidate holding their own caucus to pick the number
of delegates allotted their candidate.

In this way NDC could effectively by-pass the
winner-take-all provision of the state primary law;
but only if its uncommitted proportional slate won the
primary. In February it looked like the Democratic

primary voter would have only two choices on the ballot, the Muskie slate or the proportional slate. If Muskie's slate received the most votes, even if it was only 51% of the vote, then Muskie would get all twenty-two of Rhode Island's votes at the national Convention However, if the proportional slate received more votes, each of the Presidential candidates represented at the February 27 proportional slate convention would receive that portion of the states twenty-two delegates allotted him by the convention balloting.

The New Democratic Coalition of Rhode Island had really put something together. Even if the proportional slate did not win at the state primary, the NDC still had an ace up the sleeve - a challenge. Under Democratic national rules, any counter-slate could challenge a regular slate before the national Convention's Credentials Committee on the grounds that the regular slate failed to comply with the national directives for selecting state delegates. Nelson warned unequivocally in January that if the process for picking Muskie's slate fell short of the national rules, the proportional slate would challenge. "I think it's very likely that we will challenge them," Nelson let it be known. "These reform rules run against their grain."

The barbs were flying between Nelson and the state party regulars. When Doorley appeared to be delaying the announcement of Muskie's slate-making meeting, John reacted, making page four of the PROVIDENCE JOURNAL: "If Doorley doesn't speed things up and start telling people how they can become delegates, he could find his slate with a challenge."

The established order was in trouble. How serious, not even Doorley could yet appreciate. But the facts were that NDC would not go away. It could no longer be ignored, therefore the time had come to have it out. Doorley threw his clout in that direction: "This New

140

Democratic Coalition is chiding me for failure to call
a delegate selection meeting. It is obvious to me that
there is nothing that the Democratic organization can
do to satisfy the whimsical demands of Mr. John C.
Nelson and his cohorts. It is my sincere belief that
despite the tremendous degree of reform legislation
enacted by the General Assembly and the feeling of
reform within the party, that unless the NDC set all
the rules, they will challenge us all the way." Then
subtly characterizing Nelson in less than complimentary
terms, "You give someone the banana, the bunch, the
stalk and then the tree and they're still not happy. I
don't know what to give them." Nelson, in the topsy-
turvy language of the world of political antagonism,
couldn't have been more complimented. Doorley,
the stalwart of the closed political system, after two
years of intense NDC reform activity, had finally
publically recognized the NDC as a significant threat
to the status quo, reaching so far as to personally
insult John Nelson, that banana-eating troublemaker
of Orms Street.

February 27, 1972
Statement of Purpose
State Delegate Convention For the Proportional Slate

"This is a convention for voters of liberal persua-
sion, dedicated to the cause of making democracy work
in Rhode Island, and to securing for the rank-and-file
voter full, meaningful, and timely access to the presidential nominating process.
"Through the efforts of the New Democratic Coalition, significant reforms have already been achieved
in this state's presidential preference and delegate
selection processes. These reforms include (1) the
public delegate slating meetings occurring this week

for four Democratic and two Republican candidates; (2) the impartial positioning of delegate slates on the ballot; (3) the elimination of the asterisk showing party endorsement; (4) the elimination of the advantage of party endorsed slates in the delegate candidate petitioning process; and (5) the scheduling of a later primary to maximize voter information and choice in the presidential preference poll.

"These things add up to a much greater voice in the presidential nominating process for the ordinary voter than he was permitted in 1968. However, great obstacles still stand in the way of full and meaningful participation - notably the winner-take-all character of the primary and the 26-month rule governing party affiliation.

"Despite these significant reforms, this year's primary still denies those who support minority candidates any delegate representation in the national convention. The same party bosses are in power - this time headed by Mayor Doorley and the next party chairman, Larry McGarry. They are still determined to maintain control of the delegate selection process and by withholding information on how to become a delegate, they have effectively nullified the voice of ordinary voters, including the newly enfranchised under-21 group, so hopeful of participating this year. This year is guaranteed to be a rerun of 1968 unless new people, including many who never considered themselves Democrats, are given an effective voice in the presidential nominating process.

"The New Democratic Coalition is hosting the selection of a proportional slate of delegates today. The slate you elect will run in the May 23 primary with its members pledged in proportion to the presidential preference vote of this convention.

"Win or lose, we will send a lobbying delegation

to Miami in July to place the issue of proportional representation squarely before the nation. In no other way can the winner-take-all primary be challenged, and an effective voice be assured the supporters of minority candidates.

"The party regulars have vast resources. But we have a just cause - everyones right to be heard. "The time for sacrifice is now. The issue is clear. The stakes were never higher. Welcome - to this effort to bring democracy to the voters of our state."

The convention was held at the Rhodes-on-the-Pawtuxet auditorium. Cars were pouring into the parking lot throughout the noon hour registration. For me, it was a grand reunion. Syd was back in full force, John was running from phone, to registration table, to speaker's table, performing a three-act play in one. I recognized a dozen summer executive committee faces helping with registration and seating along with some new student staff helpers. It wasn't a huge attendance, maybe five hundred, but then Rhode Island wasn't a huge state. Nelson had done all he could to advertise, using radio broadcasts and the fair-handed writing of Providence's two political reporters Brian Dickinson of the EVENING BULLETIN and John P. Hackett of the PROVIDENCE JOURNAL. That a convention of this sort could be called was a miracle in itself, totally unprecedented in Rhode Island's far-from-liberal political history.

The convention got under way with a jolt. The issues of race and poverty were more signicant on the national level than the state level. This may well have been a consideration in choosing George W. Wiley, Director of the National Welfare Rights Organization to deliver the convention's keynote address. Wiley stepped to the podium in afro and dashiki. As if before a national

news camera, he spoke loudly with a carefully worded
militancy which struck, yet did not visibly penetrate,
the timidly smiling, middle-class audience. Wiley
brought his own audience though, a rank and raucous
cadre of welfare protest specialists; housewives on
relief mostly, fat and boisterous or gaunt and gray.
On cue, they rose from their back-row seats releasing
bursting ballons, marching down the aisles, pickets
in hand, tooting toy bugles - just like on TV. I watched
Nelson carefully. He was ashen with anguish. Our
white-collar liberals weren't expecting this. But in
a minute, the wave of tumultuous meek had subsided
and the convention went about the business of nominating Presidential candidates, balloting and selecting
delegates.

RETURN FROM EXILE

May-June 1972
    It had been nearly four years since Gene McCarthy
had extolled the exiled Grant Park Democrats to "work
within the political system and help seize control of
the Democratic Party in 1972." New reform-minded
national leaders had appeared then, rising like a phoenix
above the ashes of Hubert Humphrey's jaded "politics
of joy." Most notable was George McGovern who, as
much as any man, was responsible for the rewriting
of Party delegate selection rules. And it was to
McGovern that the tide of victory turned in the Rhode
Island '72 Democratic primary.
    Honorable Ed Muskie, the party's great white hope,
was unable to go the distance. By May 23, the date
of the Rhode Island Presidential primary, he was only
a shadow of the candidate he had once been. Rhode
Island, Muskie's backyard state, was no longer un-

contested territory. George McGovern, who in February had tacitly agreed to keep his name off the state's primary ballot, letting his interests be represented by the NDC uncommitted, proportional slate, which strongly favored him anyway, now, in May, changed his strategy. He left his name on the ballot and won, thereby scuttling the NDC proportional slate.

Nelson, the man who had personally initiated and directed party refom in Rhode Island, faithfully adhering to Senator McGovern's guidelines, now saw that same Senator,in the role of candidate, deny the one chance to attain the spirit of those guidelines. John, physically exhausted from endless hours he had devoted to NDC, now felt betrayed. He was thrice betrayed: first by McGovern who left his name on the primary ballot; then by the proportional slate delegates who resigned to become McGovern delegates; and by his own NDC organization, most conspicuously, Syd and Jack Indeck who, now in the heat of victory, discarded principle and abandoned the proportional slate joining McGovern's winner-take-all march to Miami. As Syd justified her act later, "It was a chance to win." And with the turn of events, so turned Syd's opinion of NDC. As she said retrospectively, "I think now that NDC was working too far outside established channels and when you do that there is a temptation to think that you are superior." To her, it was a choice of being "repectable" or "acceptable," and she, along with the majority of our fairweather liberals, chose the latter. John Nelson, however, insisted upon his respectability. Within a month after the primary, he resigned from the New Democratic Coalition and left Rhode Island.

Stunned and bewildered, the state party regulars, seeing their candidate defeated at the polls, scrambled vainly in the primary aftermath to hold on to their receeding power. Because McGovern had no delegation on the ballot with him, he was required to pick a slate after the primary, in consultation with the state party chairman. The new party chairman, Larry McGarry, proposed a slate chosen from the top vote-getters among the delegates on the ballot. This, of course, was heavily weighted with the big name organizational figures: Doorley, St. Germain, LaFrance and also some from the proportional slate, ironically including the name of John Nelson.

But the state McGovern forces had already drawn up their own slate consisting of twenty-two delegates and fifteen alternates, most of whom had been selected at the pre-primary McGovern caucus. McGarry rejected this slate as unrepresentative and with a slight concession, demanded, "I want at least half of the delegation from the top twenty-two on the ballot." The other slate, he insisted, "I will not certify." So the McGovern delegates caucused and in a less than conciliatory mood, offered six alternate seats to the state party leaders. McGarry, spokesman for the once all-powerful state organization, was enraged at having been thrown a bone by the McGovernites; "I will not even consider honoring the ridiculous proposal of people who have no right to make any proposal."

McGarry accused McGovern of "welshing" on a deal. He said that in a phone conversation held only twenty-four hours before the McGovern delegates made their "ridiculous" proposal, he had spoken personally with George McGovern who had agreed to split the delegates fifty-fifty, eleven to the McGovernites and eleven to the party regulars. McGarry, indignant at what he considered betrayal, described the controversial phone call as "a most amicable conversation with no ifs, ands or buts. The line was clear as a bell; the agreement was fifty-fifty, not only the dele-

146

gates, but on the alternates and the national committeeman and committeewoman." When asked about the dis-
crepancy in reports on the conversation, McGarry,
standing amidst the rubble of the organization's invincible structure, could only shake his head. "One of us,"
McGarry said gravely, "is not an honorable man, because one of us is not telling the truth."

McGarry, whose predecessor two years earlier had
ignored National Democratic Chairman Harris's letter
urging a state reform task force and who had ignored
the reform liberals of Rhode Island, was now being ignored. The chairman of the McGovern slate, Dave Evans,
certified his own delegates clearing the way for them
to participate in the Miami Democratic National Convention giving George McGovern all of Rhode Island's voice.
As Nelson summed up from the sidelines: "It is ironic
that we were locked out by the regulars in '68 when they
tossed us only two and one half votes on the national
convention delegation and this time, due to their own
dalliance and the winner-take-all primary they wrote,
they have locked themselves out one hundred per cent."

DEMOCRATS IN EXILE 1968-1972 was typeset on an
IBM Executive using Bold Face #2 type. Titles
and subtitles are photographic enlargements of the
same type. The book was printed in a small print
shop using a Davidson 233 offset press and bound
at a commercial bindery in Chicago. SOL Press
is the publisher and principal distributor. Author's
royalties from the sale of this book will be donated
to the amnesty lobby.